CW01661587

Softly, Softly

by
JOAN MOULES

Softly, Softly

The Tears Behind the Triumphs of

Ruby Murray

by
JOAN MOULES

Published by Evergreen,
PO Box 52, Cheltenham, Gloucestershire,
GL50 1YQ.

Printed in Great Britain by
Beshara Press, Cheltenham

ISBN 0 9522413 2 3

CONTENTS

List of Photographs

Introduction

Remember saying: "Let's have a Ruby Murray"? It was, of course, rhyming slang for "Let's go for a curry!" and this is the story of the girl who inspired that timeless phrase. She topped the bill at the London Palladium in the Fifties, and still delights audiences today with her *softly, softly* Irish charm.

Ruby Murray, the colleen with the husky voice, had rocketed to fame and fortune by the age of 19. They called her "the Heartbeat Girl" in those halcyon days when she became the golden songstress of the hit parade. But Ruby's story wasn't all glamour and glory; there were many sadnesses, too. In the telling of her tale to Joan Moules, Ruby has not glossed over the grey patches. She has spoken frankly about her problems, and how she overcame them, and of those who helped her.

This book tells of her rapid rise to stardom, and how she and her family coped with it. There are stories about some of the famous people with whom she worked, including Frank Sinatra, Tommy Steele, Jimmy Jewel and Ben Warriss, Patti Page, Dickie Valentine, Ronnie Hilton, David Whitfield, Harry Secombe, Frankie Laine, Norman Wisdom, Vic Oliver, Joe ("Mr. Piano") Henderson, Tommy Cooper, Ronnie Carroll and Johnnie ("Cry") Ray. There are stories, too, of the ordinary folk who took the shy young singer to their hearts and became loyal fans; stories of priests of different denominations who became her friends.

In 1955 Ruby had five records simultaneously in the Top Twenty, the accolade list of the Fifties. Remember them? *Heartbeat ... Softly, Softly ... Let Me Go, Lover ... Happy Days and Lonely Nights ... If Anyone Finds This I Love You ...* it was an achievement that earned her a place in the *Guinness Book of Theatrical Records*; an accomplishment that no-one, not even the Beatles, has beaten.

It's all here ... the happiness and heartache, the magic and the mistakes, the travels and the torments, the illusions and the inspirations. This is the story of Ruby Murray, golden girl.

Foreword by Frankie Vaughan

I first met Ruby at the Bernard Delfont agency when I was looking to make the grade as a recording star. I was searching for songs, and a friend of mine, Gerry Levine, rang to say he had a great song, but when he played it I knew it was not for me.

I knew immediately who it would suit and I told him: "There's a young girl who's just had a big hit and she's at the same office as me. Ruby Murray. Her voice is sensational, and she's the sweetest little thing you've ever seen."

The song was *Evermore*, which Ruby sang with great feeling, and pushed to the top of the hit parade. Afterwards, Ruby and I worked together on record programmes — such as Jack Payne's show *Off The Record* and *The Daily Mirror Award Show* — but she was so nervous that I was forever smoothing her down. I told her she had nothing to worry about. All she had to do was walk out there, looking great, and sing ... which she did beautifully.

I rate her voice amongst the best. It's unique, it's beautiful, and it's instantly recognisable. When you consider that this sweet girl came into showbusiness *softly, softly* when so many American stars were such punchy singers — well, it's quite remarkable.

On and off stage, she's a smashing lady; my wife and I adore her. We've had occasions to be working in the same place but at different theatres. The last time that this happened, during a summer season, we went to the races several times and got together after the show — Stella and myself, Ruby and Ray. We always had a laugh. She has a great sense of humour and is full of fun. She is also a very professional lady and I'm glad the story of her life is being told.

If I go back through the years there are showbusiness friends I've loved dearly. I count Ruby Murray among them. Her's is a fascinating story. I know you're going to love it.

Ruby Murray

CHAPTER 1

A Star is Born

Picture a pretty Irish girl on stage at the Metropolitan theatre in Edgware Road. The year was 1954, the show *Yankee Doodle Blarney*, and the pretty Irish singer was Ruby Murray.

Television producer Richard Afton was in the audience, and what he saw and heard that day sent him backstage to sign Ruby for the singing spot in the TV show *Quite Contrary*, which had just been vacated by Joan Regan who was going into variety.

Ruby was 18, going on 19, and she loved singing. Her husky voice was gentle, soothing and melodious, and she was young, fresh looking, shy — and terrified before a performance.

"My palms went sticky and my throat felt like wet cement", she recalled. The lights and the cameras frightened her, though she had already made a previous television appearance when she was 12. "But I was a child then..."

She wished she'd said No, but it was too late. Suddenly she was on. "I thought of my dad back there in Belfast, sitting by the screen and watching me. I thought of my mum, my brother Jack, and my best friend Marie, and I *knew* I couldn't let them down. I sang *Little Things Mean A Lot*, and I meant it, too. Once I was singing, then it was all right. I was happy."

Richard Afton telephoned conductor Ray Martin and asked him to watch the show, because he thought that in Ruby he had something special. Ray thought so, too, and within hours he had spoken to Ruby about trying a recording. Two days later she made a record for his company (Columbia) on which Norrie Paramor played the piano. The title was *Get Well Soon* with *Two Kinds of Tears* on the flip side.

Her second record at the beginning of 1955 was *Heartbeat*, but because of her accent it nearly became "Heartbee". Said Norrie: "We realised the final 't' was missing, but fortunately we were able to record them later on the original master."

Heartbeat was the first of her discs to sell in its thousands and Ruby became known as the "Heartbeat Girl", quickly following her success with the song that became her signature tune, *Softly, Softly*. By April of that year Ruby had five records in the Top Twenty simultaneously — *Heartbeat; Softly, Softly; Let Me Go, Lover; If Anyone Finds This, I Love You;* and *Happy Days and Lonely Nights.*

In the Fifties the *Top Twenty Record Show* on the radio was avidly listened to by young people every Sunday. Sometimes both sides of a recording were in the charts in their own right. This was because dealers' returns were based on the side of the disc for which the customer asked. Although, of course, the two numbers comprising the entire record were sold, the idea was to indicate the selling power of an individual song.

In three months Ruby's records topped 650,000 sales. One review read: "Up and down the country they are falling for teenager Ruby Murray, the singing strawberry blonde from Belfast's Donegal Road, who is climbing to fame as the 'Heartbeat Girl'. Already she topples the giants of disc and leads the parade of best-sellers."

She was still in *Quite Contrary* on television, and another review from the same period asked: "Why has this Ruby such a sparkle? When she looks out of the TV screen she has the freshness of a summer breeze. Her eyes twinkle with an Irish impishness and her wide smile makes you want to be her friend. Team this with her shy sincerity and you have part of the secret of Ruby Murray's success. She is completely natural."

Headlines like "Biggest success story in showbusiness this year is shy, modest Ruby Murray, a second Vera Lynn" dominated the entertainment pages. Vera Lynn said: "Nobody wants to be a *second* anyone", and Ruby smiled and told reporters: "If I last as long (as Vera) I'll be grateful." Ruby's Irish brogue and

Vera's London accent were the differences. The similarity was in the warmth of both personalities and what one reviewer called "the heart-tugging emotion and sincerity" in their voices.

The Beverley Sisters, who first saw Ruby on *Quite Contrary*, were certain from the start that she was star material. "We were enchanted, absolutely knocked out", said Joy Beverley.

* * * *

Ruby was the youngest of Winifred and Daniel Murray's four children. She was born in Belfast on 29th March, 1935 and christened Ruby Florence Campbell Murray. Her parents were friendly with a local comedienne who played the Empire theatre in Belfast, where they went every time they could afford it.

This comedienne was a big woman, weighing around 20 stone, and she came on stage wearing a tutu, a huge bow, and heavy boots. In the daytime she worked at the local fish-and-chip shop and always added a few extra chips to Winnie's order when she was expecting the baby. "For little Ruby", she used to say, and when the blue-eyed, flaxen-haired child was born, Winnie and Dan ("Big Dan" as he was known around Belfast) named her after Ruby Florence Campbell, fish-and-chip shop assistant and comedienne.

The middle and late Fifties were a time of great change. Although the war had been over for a decade many wartime conditions still prevailed. The young ones began to come into their heyday; it was the time for angry young men, such as John Osborne who wrote *Look Back In Anger* and John Braine, who wrote *Room At The Top*.

In 1955, the year of Ruby's first great recording successes, Ruth Ellis was the last woman to be hanged in Britain (for murdering her lover), and the first nuclear power station was opened (at Calder Hall). Most young people lived at home; not many could afford a flat in those days, and in any case their parents wouldn't have thought it right. Ordinary young people were still very much within the family circle — they seldom broke away to do their own thing, however much they wanted to, because of circumstances and the general conventions of the time. Most of them left home only when they married, unless there were other domestic or work reasons.

Television was in its infancy. It began just before the war but was halted from 1939 until hostilities ceased. It took a while to get going again. Ruby and a host of other young singers and comedians came along in time for the first television boom.

When she came over from Ireland with *Yankee Doodle Blarney*, theatrical agent Philip Solomon was handling her affairs. As well as the television show, he booked her for a tour in which trumpeter Kenny Baker was top of the bill. Philip Solomon then sold her contract to Keith Devon of the Delfont agency. Keith vividly recalls the day Ruby and her mother came to see him, and Winnie, who was always the spokeswoman, asked if he would consider being Ruby's agent.

Keith, along with Bernard Delfont and Billy Marsh, was a partner in the agency. He replied that he couldn't possibly take on Ruby without hearing her sing and asked where she was working. She told him: "Bradford, but we haven't got the fare", so he gave them £15 and said he'd come and see her as soon as he could. A few weeks later he caught her act at the Finsbury Park Empire in London: "I thought she was the best girl vocalist I'd heard and I negotiated for the contract."

Philip Solomon would sell only the stage contract, and not the recording one, but Keith had so much faith in Ruby's talent that he bought it anyway. Within a few months he was able to buy the recording one, too.

Comedienne Audrey Jeans, already under contract to Keith Devon, became a close friend when Keith asked her to take Ruby under her wing. First she introduced Ruby to dress designer St. John Roper who created beautiful unfussy gowns which enhanced her fresh and simple charm. Audrey also advised her on make-up; Ruby at this time was using heavier stage make-up than her delicate skin required. "In fact, away from the lights I looked a bit like a Red Indian", she recalled, "but I had faith in Keith and did as I was told. He was a very warm and humorous man, and he always made me laugh, which made conforming easy."

On the same bill on that tour was a group called The Four Ramblers. Although Ruby wasn't down with the "wines and spirits", as those in small print at the bottom of the bill are called, they were higher than she was. One of them was Val Doonican — and listening to his easy, happy voice, romantic Ruby immediately became infatuated. Val already had a girl friend, so Ruby contented herself with watching him, listening and dreaming about him.

Val was at that time studying the classical guitar. In one lot of digs was a rocking chair. He used to sit in it and rock while studying, and eventually a rocking chair became part of his act. Val recalls that tour and the first time he met Ruby. "She seemed so young and innocent", he said, "Almost as if she shouldn't be out alone."

Her next date was in Durham but The Four Ramblers (and Val) wouldn't be there. So kind-hearted Val telephoned a friend of his, Catholic priest Father John Caden, and asked him to look after Ruby. Then he gave her Father John's address and told her to see him and he would make sure she was all right. The priest introduced her to Val's landlady and she found her digs.

Father John attended Ruby's concerts whenever he could and generally kept a fatherly eye on her, even bringing her little snacks to eat because she was so thin and pale. "I looked wan, but in fact I was as strong as an ox", she says. "People often thought I was sickening for something because I had so little colour in my cheeks. I used to tell them, 'I'm not as fragile as I seem.'"

Twelve Sunday concerts were arranged with Harold Fielding, and it was just about this time that her records were released and shot into the hit parade. Ruby was earning £100 a concert but Keith negotiated for more money, telling Harold: "You can't have her for that now, she's a hot property."

Keith also secured her first top-of-the-bill date, at the Bristol Hippodrome in March 1955. The reviews in those early days commented on her stage walk-on. To this day Ruby is hesitant as she comes forward, but then it was much more pronounced. Some of the critics found it endearing but others found it annoying. She was criticised for her "childlike stage manner" and urged to get more confidence. "She has no stage presence at all", said one critic.

Getting on and off stage is always difficult, and everyone has to work out their own method. George Robey used to run on and Gracie Fields came on singing; she had, in effect, already begun in the wings.

Ruby admitted that she needed pushing — not physically, but verbally. The hardest bit was in getting from the wings to the microphone. She says: "It's like waiting to go to the dentist. You're not sure whether you're going to make a mistake, or whether the band is, or if the mike is going to fail or the lights go off. All these things go through your mind because it's not a job where you pull a handle and it comes out the same every day. It's *totally* different every time and for every performance, for both you and the audience. Somewhere you'll go well and somewhere else you could die. But once you actually reach the mike, and you feel your audience like you and you like them and everything's going smoothly, you can relax and enjoy it."

Comedian Jimmy Wheeler was used as anchor man for Ruby's first top-of-the-bill at Bristol Hippodrome in case she wasn't a big enough box office draw. He said afterwards: "How much did her name mean in Bristol? That was the question, and because it was an unsolved query Keith Devon wanted me to be an anchor on the same bill. Of course I said yes. My act does not need a band rehearsal, so I didn't arrive in Bristol until the Monday afternoon. I was astonished to find a great queue for the box office, half way round the theatre. Richard Afton's presentation of Ruby on television and her subsequent recordings had been enough to get Bristol alive with excitement, and her first top-of-the-bill appearance was a great success. No anchor was needed."

Her discs stayed in the Top Twenty to create a theatrical record that still stands, and earned her a place in the *Guinness Book of Theatrical Records.* Yet still the critics carped. One said: "She has the hardest job in the world, being boosted right to the top and then having to learn the rudiments of the job. Learning to move and feel at ease on huge stages has been only one of her problems."

He was totally wrong. Ruby's "overnight" success had been devised many years before. She had served her apprenticeship on various stages — large, small and makeshift — in touring shows, first in Ireland and later throughout the length and breadth of Britain, while she was still a child.

CHAPTER 2

Home and Away

The "overnight" success actually began on the kitchen table of 84 Moltick Street, Donegal Road, Belfast, when Ruby was two or three years old, and her father, Dan Murray, realised she could sing. She remembers being lifted on to the scrubbed wooden table and singing for her dad and his mates. "He was the love of my life, my protector. He always believed in me", she said.

Dan was born in Sixth Street off Belfast's Shankill Road. He came of Scottish stock; his parents were from Kilbirnie, Ayrshire, but he was born in Ireland. He had four brothers and one sister. His mother died very young and his father, an Army man, was a harsh disciplinarian with the family. Perhaps he needed to be, bringing them up alone.

Years later Ruby's sisters Patsy and Lilian decided to research the Murray family tree. They discovered that two of the brothers had gone to Canada. John Murray was shot, rum-running across the Canadian and American border during Prohibition. Billy Murray married three times in Ireland, at different times, his first wife presenting him with ten children before she died. He then married her sister, with whom he had another ten. And when she died he married yet again and had another four.

The children were called John the first, John the second and so on... the same names in each family. But Billy ran out of ideas when he reached the final little girl — he called her Pinky! Widowed for the third time, he joined his brother in Canada, married an Indian squaw and became an alcoholic! Patsy and Lilian gave up when they got that far...

Daniel ran away from home and joined the Army when he was 16. He borrowed a friend's identity card to get in because he was under age. His first posting was to India and later he regaled his family with tales of that seemingly romantic land. He spent 12 years in the Royal Inniskilling Fusiliers, then became storeman for the Royal Engineers at the Victoria Barracks, Belfast.

He loved all his children but adored Ruby. She was the youngest and from a tender age fulfilled his longings for the stage. She was, in her own words, "blonde, bubbly, a bit like Shirley Temple then, and very precocious".

She couldn't have been more than four when her parents took her to see G.H. Elliott, "the chocolate-coloured coon", at the Empire theatre, Belfast, and after that his songs went into her rapidly growing repertoire. That was also the occasion which made her want to sing in a theatre herself one day. Although too young to explain it, she knew that the plush curtains, the warmth and smell of the place and, above all, the happy atmosphere would draw her back again and again.

Ruby's mother, Winifred, lived in Seventh Street, and it was her brother who was the friend from whom Dan borrowed the identity card to get into the Army. When he returned he went to live with her parents, Annie and Billy Connelly, and began to court their daughter, Winnie.

Annie, Winnie's mother, was Annie Rooney before her marriage, and Winifred's baptismal name was Wilhelmina. So with Annie Rooney and Billy Connelly, Daniel, Wilhelmina and the Irish, Scots and Canadian elements in her background, Ruby Florence Campbell Murray was a gorgeous mixture.

Winifred's mother Annie Rooney, Ruby's maternal grandmother, had 12 children, but six had died from TB before reaching adulthood. The eldest daughter, Lilian, went to Canada in service with a wealthy Jewish family. Annie pawned everything she could to get the money to give her a chance, and Lilian took that chance with both hands. She worked hard and willingly and when she eventually left service she became a hairdresser, with the help and blessing of the family for whom she worked. After a few years she had enough money saved to send for two of her sisters, which she did, and first Meg, then Winnie, prepared to leave their homeland for the promise of a new life in Canada.

When it was Winnie's turn she was aged 14. She was the quietest of the family, very shy but very pretty, with jet black hair and round, rosy Irish cheeks. Annie didn't want to send her in a shawl, and her idea of what 14-year-olds wore in Canada was a grey suit, a fox fur and a picture hat. To obtain these luxury items she worked as a district nurse and took on extra jobs like scrubbing the stage at the Empire, the same stage her grand-daughter would later grace. So Winnie would go to Canada, looking as smart as Annie could make her.

An acquaintance of Annie's was travelling on the boat at the same time and promised to keep an eye on young Winnie, who wasn't sure if she was excited or frightened (or both) by the great adventure. She travelled by boat and train and arrived at Toronto station where big sister Lilian was due to meet her. Waiting at the station for her young sister, Lilian watched anxiously as everyone descended from the train. No Winnie. She strode up and down the platform looking for her and muttering: "Winnie, oh where *are* you, Winnie?" And every time she passed, Winnie, sitting sedately on the bench in her fox fur and picture hat, said in a tiny whisper: "Lil, Lil, it's me. I'm here." Eventually Lilian looked down. "Oh my God", she said, "Get into a car quick before everyone sees you."

When Winnie got back to the house there seemed to be dozens of cousins and second cousins there, and they all fell about laughing. Lilian found her some suitable clothes and they passed hers around the family that evening, saying: "Gee, is this what they *really* wear in Ireland?"

Lilian had found her a job with another Jewish family, but during her first week Winnie almost got the sack because she went round the house blowing out the candles that were lit for the Jewish Sabbath. Her employers appealed to her sister: "Gee, Lil, doesn't your sister know *anything*?"

She returned to Ireland a few years later, settled back into family life, and she and "Big Dan" Murray, who was then lodging with her parents, were married.

Their first child, Jack, was born in April 1929 and Winnie went back to Canada again, this time with her husband and son. She went into service in Toronto and Dan became a security guard for a construction company. They stayed long enough to have two more children, Patsy and Lilian, then returned home because Annie Rooney was dying. They left two-year-old Lilian there to be brought up by her aunt of the same name, and boarded the ship to bring them back to the old country with the other two children, Jack and Patsy.

Ruby was born at 84 Moltick Street at five minutes to twelve on 29th March, 1935, but there were complications at the birth and an ambulance, hastily summoned, took mother and baby to hospital where it was sorted out and she was officially registered at ten minutes past twelve, on 30th March. Either way it makes her an Aries subject, but she always celebrates her birthday on the 29th.

She remembers living in Moltick Street and waiting for her father to come home from work. "He was a docker then, and always used to put me on the crossbar of his bike and take me for a ride round before going in for tea", she recalled. She also always sat at his right hand at the table, and thought there was no-one in the world like her dad. As she grew older and recognised that he wasn't the super being her childish imagination had conjured up, she loved him just as much. They shared a passion for the theatre and animals that kept them close throughout his life — in spite of other differences later when Ruby married.

His love of animals led to him bringing home a greyhound once. "I got it cheap", he said. He kept it in the yard and called it 'Desert Star'. "Me mother had to get a job to keep it in food", Ruby laughed, "and it never won a race."

When visitors came to the house, Ruby used to sing for them. "No way would I let them out without singing a song. Everyone absolutely hated me, and now I can understand why.

One uncle used to throw cushions at me and say, 'Oh, you're terrible!' but I went on singing and Dan went on encouraging me."

When war broke out in 1939 Ruby was aged four-and-a-half, and later she remembers being pushed under the settee when the bombers were heard overhead. Soon after her fifth birthday she was evacuated to the country with her brother and sister. They went to a farm near Bush Mills, and for Ruby it was to be the unhappiest period of her childhood.

The farmer and his wife found Jack and Patsy docile enough, but couldn't stand Ruby. She was too outrageous for them and they decided to knock it out of her and make her "normal". They disciplined her harshly, and beat her whenever she said or did anything out of place — but treated her brother and sister reasonably. Coming from the spoilt atmosphere of a doting father and kindly mother, poor Ruby was bewildered and frightened. The others were too young to realise fully what was happening, and in any case too frightened to tell tales when their parents came for their fortnightly visits. The farmer and his wife locked Ruby into a shed with a pony one night when she had "misbehaved", and she was terrified because she saw and heard the rats running about.

Then one day she was bitten by a cleg (a horsefly). Her leg became poisoned, and, to give them their due, the farm couple treated it as they would have for one of their own children. They put red-hot bread poultices on it, which had Ruby screaming for mercy, and that, of course, made them even harsher with her. Possibly they, too, were frightened when they saw the state of her leg. But their answer was more poultices to draw out the poison, and never mind the pain. Then the poison began to travel up her leg, and a red line appeared. They put a bandage on and when Dan and Winnie came for their visit told them she had simply been bitten by a fly and that the bandage was to protect it and stop dirt from getting in. None of the children said a word because it was very much a house where you were seen and not heard, which was one of the reasons why the couple disliked Ruby. She was far too exuberant for their liking. However she was growing quieter and more introverted every day. For the first time in her young life she knew that not everyone was going to love her, and it hurt.

"They wanted to change me", she said, "and they did, they really did. They tried to tame me and I became totally frightened of people. From being a bubbly, obnoxious little girl who wanted to sing for everybody I became a loner."

The pain from the bite just added to the sadness of being away from those she loved, and who loved her. She was too young to worry about what it was doing to her leg, only to feel the pain and know she *mustn't* cry out or she would be punished for making a fuss.

On their next visit her leg was still bandaged and Dan and Winnie were told: "It's doing fine". But Dan wasn't satisfied. He sensed something was wrong, not so much from the bandage around his daughter's leg as from the change in her attitude. She seemed to have lost all her spirit, all her nerve and vivacity. They had their usual taxi to the station, and Dan suddenly said: "Something's terribly wrong there, I'm going back", and they returned to the farm.

Ruby was in the tin bath, and of course the bandage was off her leg. Dan took one look and in Ruby's words: "He went berserk. He wrapped me in a blanket and took me there and then, without clothes or anything, in the taxi back home. He left Jack and Patsy there, because they assured him they were fine, but not long afterwards they also came home."

Dan had caught the poisoned leg just in time. If it had gone gangrenous she would have lost her leg. As it was, it took a long time to heal and the mental damage never completely left her. It changed her into a nervous, weepy child, who became afraid of doing the things which were natural to her. Gradually, of course, she grew less timid, but the fright within remained for many, many years.

CHAPTER 3

The Show Rolls On

The evacuation episode had a traumatic effect on Ruby. "I was afraid of people after that, I never trusted them", she said. But apart from that, and one other happening, Ruby's childhood memories are mostly happy.

The other event concerned Dan's youngest brother, Jim. "I remember my Uncle Jimmy when he was in the Army, came home on leave from France a couple of times and took us out. He would line the three of us up against the door and say 'Now I'm taking you into town today, and what is it before we go?' And we chorused together 'No wants, no wants, Uncle Jimmy. We won't want *anything*.' And we got into town and we wanted everything, and he bought us everything. He was a wonderful man, soft and gentle, and he was killed at Dunkirk.

"I remember playing on the doorstep and all the blinds being drawn, and going up to my father's bedroom and he was crying. I'd never seen him cry before. That sticks in my mind.

"Mostly, though, I recall the comfort, the family comfort. I remember going out on a frosty night. We children were always sent on messages, and I remember on a cold, winter night going down to the shop, then coming out into the freezing air and going back to the warmth and the lights, the comfort of home. No telly, just my parents and a couple of friends sitting around; but it was such a secure feeling when you came in out of the cold.

"I remember one occasion when Patsy and I had been sent to buy a cake because we had visitors. We chose a sponge cake, with lots of jam in the middle, and on our way home we began to fight.

"Patsy was carrying the cake and I was teasing her about

something when she said, 'If you say that once more I'm going to let you have this right in the kisser.' I replied, 'I shall tell my daddy on you', knowing Dan would stick up for me. She lifted the cake and took careful aim. I didn't even duck and, bang, there was the jammy sponge exactly where she said it would be. When we'd stopped laughing, the enormity of the situation hit us, and we scraped it all carefully from my face and patted it back together into some semblance of a cake.

"It didn't look too bad, only a little squashed. But we were both sent to bed for giggling when it was being eaten and enthused over. After all, we couldn't tell them why we were laughing!"

When Patsy was eight, and Ruby six, Dan bought them some little stage outfits and they worked together on different routines. "Patsy was always laughing and treating it as a huge joke, but even then I was taking it seriously and insisting Patsy practised and rehearsed to get it right".

When Dan got a better job in the Civil Service they moved to Benbow Street and Ruby went to Fane Street school. She hated school and was very glad to leave. Having become so much a loner she didn't make friends easily — although the one girl she did become close to had a piano and Ruby used to go to her house as often as possible. Later the Murrays bought a piano themselves, for 30 shillings, and Ruby happily played and sang every second she was in the house. She went to music lessons about this time, but never learned to read music. To this day she plays by ear.

Then Sydney Donnelly came into her life. He owned a drapers on the Shankill Road. Anyone who had a shop and a house, as he did, was a multi-millionaire in the young Ruby's eyes. But more important to her was the fact that he could read music. Dan arranged for him to go through the written copies of songs with her and if they were too high, which they often were because of her low register, to write them in the key in which she should sing them to make them comfortable for her voice. Ruby recalls with great joy the hours spent with him setting keys. "He was covered in fag ash", she says, "but totally absorbed in the job. He was a gorgeous man and a great milestone in my life."

Gus Hughes was the Boys Brigade teacher at Sunday School; brother Jack used to go to Boys Brigade. Gus was also the local printer and the man who ran the shows at the church. He used to book Ruby regularly, and with Sydney's copies of music she was as happy as anyone could be.

Her father also put on shows, in partnership with Jim Kirkwood and John Graham, and they called them the *KGM Shows* (their initials). Doing the job in style, they booked the Ulster Hall, which was the largest, grandest venue they could get in Belfast. Dan used to book all the local talent, putting Ruby at the top of the bill because she was his daughter and he knew she was the best.

To perform in the show everyone had to sell a hundred tickets. Dan never paid anyone (not even Ruby); they all counted it a privilege to be in the show. They sold the tickets to aunts, uncles, nieces, nephews, parents, cousins, friends and neighbours. If a tramp had money they'd sell him one, too. And it was always sold out — not a vacant seat. Dan would pay for the hall and the next day he'd go out and gamble his share of the money. He was a heavy gambler whenever he had anything to gamble with.

The shows at the Ulster Hall, and at the church hall, and all the other local ones she did while still at school, were marvellous training for what was to follow.

She left school when she was 14, "I wasn't very good at lessons", she says now. "I was always dreaming. I lived in my dreams." Looking through some old school reports, under "Ability in any special subject" it was always "Singing".

But doing shows in the evenings and at weekends was one thing; earning a living was another. And she *had* to find work. The first job was in a bakery, and she was shown how to work the jam tart machine.

"You put the dough on with your left hand, it went round,

than a stumper thing came down and put the wee crinkles on, and the next one put the jam in. So all I had to do was to put the dough on, take out the filled jam tarts and put them on a baking sheet ready to go in the oven.

"I was good at it for ten minutes, then everything went to pieces and I couldn't get them on or off quickly enough. I screwed up the whole machine. I really *jammed* it up!"

They took her off that after about half-an-hour while they unravelled the mess. Then they put her on to smelling eggs! They needed the eggs for the sponge cakes and in those days eggs weren't graded. Ruby's job was to crack them, smell them and, if they were all right, to put them in a big silver churn. She was fired from that job, too. "I was always such a dreamer", she says, "and I think I let one or two bad ones in. I know it took me years to be able to face eating an egg again."

Her next job was in a handkerchief factory and she hated that. All the workers were on piecework and she had 16 dozen hankies to hem.

"You were only accepted in the factory if you got the needle through your finger", she said, "Well, I'm not keen on pain and needles, and I thought 'I don't care whether they initiate me or not'. So I used to hold the hankies out as far away as possible, which, of course, slowed the job up, but ensured I never got a needle through my finger. After a month I got the sack. But before that I was supposed to bring a handkerchief home. All the girls did. It was part of the job, almost a tradition, to make one and smuggle it out, boxes of them sometimes. I jibbed at doing it until the last week and ashamedly, rather than proudly, I presented my mother with my 'foreigner'. She held it up, a fraying, thread-hanging piece of linen that would never have got past the fierce forewoman anyway. 'I don't know why you bothered', she said wearily."

After that Ruby went to work in a sweetshop and fared better. Meeting the public was more her cup of tea, and as she was singing in shows every weekend she was happy. Each Saturday night took her to a different town or village, a different stage. "It was wonderful", she says, "Show people always seemed to be laughing and bringing happiness and I knew that was where I wanted to be."

Cabaret artiste Bert Shaw-Cowan met her on a Saturday night in 1946, in the Seamen's Club. Ruby was an 11-year-old schoolgirl and Bert a 16-year-old seaman. Another girl, Helen Carter, was on the same bill. She sang and danced, and there was a lot of friendly rivalry between the girls.

Bert, who had been a child performer himself, left the sea the following year and went back on stage. He recalled: "I enrolled with a dance teacher called Tom Corrigan, and again met Ruby who was taking singing lessons from Tom at his studio in Royal Avenue, Belfast. I also started to get bookings as a song-and-dance man, and eventually switched to comedy and compering. I worked many times with both Ruby and Helen on a show called *Top Flight Stars*. When we were in Londonderry Ruby and her mam, who always travelled with her, stayed in my home."

Top Flight Stars lived up to its name because several performers did reach the top of the showbiz tree. One was tenor Niall Murray, who featured as a solo artiste as well as singing with a country and western group called "Pat and His Saddle Pals". Another was Charlie Sherrard, who changed his name to Patrick Haghan, and whose son is now working as Johnnie Logan, twice winner of the Eurovision Song Contest.

Then there was Joe McLaughlin, who as Josef Locke was known throughout the world; Ronnie Carroll, who was Ronnie Cleghorn and lived in the next street to Ruby; Carmel Quinn, who became a great hit in America, and The Nolans, who were billed as "The Singing Sweethearts" and are the parents of the Nolan Sisters. And there was Ruby herself, who only a few years later was to be top of the bill at theatres throughout England, Scotland, Ireland and Wales.

When Glasgow comedian Tommy Morgan was in Belfast he held auditions for his summer show. Ruby was still only 14 and her variety of jobs since leaving school had lasted weeks rather than months. She put up her age to 16 and used her sister's name, Pat Murray, because legally she was under age to go touring. But she passed the audition and arrangements were made for her and her mother to leave Belfast for the six months the show usually ran at the Glasgow Pavilion.

Her parents' marriage was not the made-in-heaven kind, though they provided such a happy home for the children, and her mother welcomed the idea of a bit of travel. The only problem was money, because Ruby wouldn't be paid until the show began and there were two weeks of rehearsals to get through first. The problem was solved by a neighbour who suggested they stay with her sister in Glasgow while they looked around for digs.

Tommy Morgan was the star of the show. Ruby says he was a hard guv'nor but he taught her much. Although she had been doing shows around Northern Ireland since she was about 10 this was her first proper costumed show, and she was eager to learn all she could.

Billed as Pat Murray (and to this day some of the folk who were in that show with her call her "Pat") she and her mother were almost penniless until that first wage packet. However, they needed somewhere to live and they couldn't stay too long with their neighbour's sister; so they tramped the streets searching for cheap, but reasonably comfortable, rooms.

"Mostly they were in the back streets", Ruby remembers. They settled for one room eventually. It was furnished with a lumpy double bed, a cooker with two flat rings and a grill, a table and two chairs. The last people to inhabit it had left behind a loaf of bread, half an onion and a wee bit of lard. The rent, in advance, had taken the rest of their money, so Winnie set to and fried the onion, put it between two slices of bread and gave it to Ruby.

"And because I was so hungry I've never tasted anything more delicious in my life", said Ruby. "If you had offered me roast duckling it couldn't have tasted any better."

The show got under way and Ruby, who had one song to

sing, went down reasonably well, but when she came off Tommy Morgan used to say: "When are you going to do something with those hands? Use them! *Feel* the song! And your hair, it looks so dry from the front. Get something to put a bit of shine on it."

And what did Ruby do? She cried. "I always cried if anyone shouted at me in those days", she recalled, "but I took his advice to heart, got some grease from the chemist for my hair and practised in front of the mirror to do something with my hands. Eventually he said 'You'll do'. That was praise indeed from him."

Even then Ruby had no great ambition to be famous. All she wanted to do was sing for the people, and be involved in the comradeship of theatre folk. And although throughout that tour she had to remain on the fringe of the social scene, because of her age, she remembers it with great affection. One of the stories she tells is of Friday lunchtimes at Lorder's pub. Friday was pay day and all the pros went there.

"At 14 I wasn't allowed in, even for a lemonade, but they used to take my mum in. God love her, she had a hard time. They'd buy her a sherry, then another sherry, and of course, in such a lot of ways I was still a child, I'd get bored and look round the door and ask, 'Are you coming, mummy?' There were two male dancers there who took this as their cue, and they used to turn to the ordinary people in the bar saying, 'Isn't that terrible, missus? Look at this poor wee child out here, and her mother at the bar drinking.' Then I'd poke my head round again and say plaintively, 'Are you coming, mummy?' She blushed easily and she'd turn on the dancers telling them to stop, and of course it made them do it all the more. 'Isn't that a disgrace, missus?' they'd say, 'That poor wee child working all the week to keep her mother in drink', and she'd finish her sherry quickly to stop their nonsense."

That Scottish season gave Ruby the wider experience of a bigger touring show. And it helped to build her confidence. She now knew she could have a life in showbusiness amongst the people she found so easy to understand and love.

They returned to Ireland at the end of the six months and Ruby auditioned for a Vic Oliver show. She was turned down. However she already had a place in *Holiday Express*, and it was in this show that Ruby met Marie Cunningham, and they became instant and inseparable friends. Wherever one was, so was the other.

"One of our big thrills in those days was to buy a tin of peaches and a small carton of cream, return to our digs and eat them. It seemed like sheer luxury."

Another afternoon frolic was to hire bicycles and with Dorrie Marr, another girl from the show, to cycle four miles to Ballyshannon and go to the local music shop, Quigleys. There the three of them would play the piano and sing for a couple of hours, to the delight of the customers.

"Marie was a Catholic and I a Protestant, but that's never made any difference to me. I would go to the Protestant service in the morning and the Catholic one with Marie in the evening, which confused many of our friends." The Murrays were Protestant; Dan, to quote his daughter, was "a very, very Orange Protestant".

The company toured Northern Ireland in a hired lorry, putting the show on in church halls, barns and anywhere where people would pay to come. In each village they tried to borrow a piano (otherwise it was Marie and her accordion for accompaniment) and often the only available piano was in the church and they had to ask the priest. Ruby remembers an old priest looking into the lorry and asking: "How many of you belong to the true church and how many are not Catholics?" They pushed her down under a pile of blankets and told him: "All you can see are in the church, Father", and they got their piano.

"Because I was the only Proddie (Protestant) in the company they used to tease me, but it was all very good-natured. There were never any incidents. Our common bond was the show and the companionship we shared."

The farmers used to come to the show on market day and, naturally enough, they brought their cows with them. Once Ruby had to fight her way to the stage door through a herd of forty cows. Another time a crowd of them got in and stood in the stalls. "The louder I sang, the louder they mooed."

Marie was a soprano and one day, sitting on the beach, she started singing *Turra Lurra Lurra* in her pale, silvery voice. Ruby joined in with what she calls her rubber-and-pebble contralto, and they both liked the sound it produced. They enjoyed doing it so much they decided to try it in the show that evening. Without telling their boss they went on together and brought the house down. For the rest of that tour the harmonising was kept in, each of them forgoing one of their solos to be able to include it.

The third one who teamed with Marie and Ruby for a while was called Dorothy. She, too, was a soprano, but they all helped with everything — selling tickets, showing people to their seats, washing up; whatever needed doing they all mucked in and did.

Dorothy used to talk about her nanny in Scotland, and when the show was in Donegal she met a boy and fell in love. One day she announced to the company that her nanny in Scotland was dying and she had to go to her. They were all sad she was leaving, and the entire company went to the station with her; they even had the bagpipes out and piped her through the street to the station, singing and, in Ruby's case at least, crying also with the emotion of it all, *Will Ye No Come Back Again?* The train puffed out of the little station to a great waving of hands and handkerchiefs — and Dorothy got off four miles farther on and went to her boyfriend in Donegal!

The piper in the show, Ken Lomond, used to walk three fields from the hall because he needed to tune up before he went on. The cows always ambled across and gathered round to look and listen.

Those same cows were contentedly chewing the cud in the first field one day until the girls hung their washing on the line they had fixed up outside. They each had one bra and two pair of knickers, and it was Ruby's turn to collect them. Humming to herself, she walked over to the line and a forlorn sight greeted her. The cows had chewed their lingerie and they were left with half a bra, and several half-pairs of knickers between them. "We had no money and no fame, but such a lot of fun", Ruby says in retrospect.

When that tour finished Marie got a job in a music shop, Solomon and Levers, owned by agent Philip Solomon's father, and she soon became manageress.

Ruby looked up to Marie: "She was bright and great with her mind even then", she says. "I knew I'd need to find something, and my greatest dream was that it would be in show-business."

One day Philip told Marie he was looking for a singer to go out on tour with a show called *Yankee Doodle Blarney*, and Marie suggested Ruby. She auditioned, and eventually the choice was between her and a girl from Dublin called Jackie Flood (who later became Jackie Lee of The Raindrops). Ruby was offered the job and thus joined the cast of *Yankee Doodle Blarney*.

CHAPTER 4

"Meet Frankie Laine ..."

It was *Yankee Doodle Blarney* that first took Ruby Murray to the south of Ireland on tour. Dan lectured her for an hour before she left the house because he was frightened she would return a Catholic! "You're very impressionable", he said, "you get to the south and they're going to try to change your religion." Ruby told him it didn't matter to her what religion people were. They were people. Church mattered, but not the way of it. "My dear father", she says now. "He was so bigoted."

Down south the first people she met outside the show were two Catholic priests. "I was 16 and they were around 60", she says, "and I immediately fell in love with them. They were Father Arthur McLean and Father Tom Doherty, and they used to make me laugh! Again I was the only Protestant in the company and everyone used to take the mickey out of me. But it was all good fun, and the two priests were great characters who loved the stage. They used to come round after the show had finished, and dress up. One played the piano and the other sang, and they joined in with everything. Father Arthur taught me to sing *Ave Maria* in Latin, and much later I recorded this." When it was time to leave, Ruby was in tears again. She asked Father Arthur to come and see her when he came to Belfast and he promised he would do so. The show moved on and the following year — on 12th July, Orange Day — he arrived. Let Ruby tell the story in her husky Irish voice and you can better picture the scene:

"All the street was decorated in red, white and blue, especially our house, my father being such a devout Orangeman. There's a ring at the bell and me mother answers the door. 'Ruby! Jesus, there's a Catholic priest at the door, he must be one of your friends', she says.

"I rushed down and threw my arms around him, saying 'You came, you came, Father Arthur', and he said, 'Yes, I know, but you shouldn't have gone to all this trouble... all these decorations just for me!' And he came in and even won my dad over with his humour and charm."

A Scotsman called Jimmy did the art posters for the show. He seemed to have no family and was very much a loner. He got on well with all the company, although he didn't mix much. One lunchtime, John Davey, who was in charge, sent Ruby and Marie round to his digs to see where he was. "He should have been here at eleven o'clock", he said.

The two girls went to the digs, and as nobody locked their doors in Ireland in those days, they went in and called out but there was neither sign nor sound. They went upstairs to his room — and there he was dead in bed. It scared the living daylights out of them both. They fled back to the hall, "as though the devil himself was after us", and told John that Jimmy was dead. They couldn't find any relatives, or indeed anyone belonging to him at all. So the company collected enough money themselves to give him a decent burial. Checking with his landlady, they discovered he was a Protestant (Ruby wasn't the only one after all) and they bought him a coffin and all turned out, with four of the men carrying the coffin up the hill to the Protestant church.

It was closed during the day and they couldn't find the minister, so they took Jimmy to the first pub and laid him across the seats. Ruby and Marie were there too, both under age to go in legally, but they did, and had soft drinks. All the men had pints of Guinness and beer, and were leaning on the coffin and resting their drinks on it saying, "Well here's to you, Jimmy, until we can find the vicar!"

"I was a bit worried", Ruby said. "It seemed rather irreverent somehow, but one of the men patted me on the shoulder saying, 'Jimmy's OK in there, an' *he* doesn't mind'."

Back in Belfast for the weekend, Ruby went shopping with her parents and called into the record shop, where Philip

Solomon asked her to take a message to Billy Livingstone, who was in the company but was compering *The Frankie Laine Show* at the Hippodrome, starring the American singer.

Ruby was wearing a skirt and jumper. "It was nothing very smart and I felt rather scruffy", she says, but she went round to the stage door and pushed her way through the crowds waiting to see the star. The stage doorman, who knew her, let her in, and she gave Billy the message: "Our bus is leaving from outside the City Hall at nine o'clock in the morning."

Billy asked if she would like to meet Frankie Laine, and she said: "Are you kidding? Yes, I would!" He took her up to his dressing room where the star was signing autographs. Frankie Laine asked her what she did and when she told him she sang, he said: "*You sing?* With a voice like that? Have you got a cold?" Ruby's huskiness, which sounds so pleasant, has caused her many problems explaining that, no, she doesn't have a cold; she just speaks like that.

Frankie then turned to his musical director, the late and great pianist and writer Carl Fisher, and asked him to take her into the other room and let her sing something. Ruby chose *Summertime* by George Gershwin and when they came out Carl Fisher said something to Frankie that she couldn't hear. He turned to her and smiled. "Carl says you're going to be good. Would you like to come to supper with us?"

Ruby says now: "I was only 16 and I'm in this awful twinset and skirt, and you know how conscious you are of your clothes at that age. Then there was the family, especially my father. Although I knew I was his favourite, and never got the cuffs round the ear the others sometimes did, I was always more scared of him than Patsy and Jack. I said: 'I'm sorry I can't, my Daddy's expecting me home, but thank you very much.'

"He said: 'That's fine. That's OK.' And I'm thinking to myself, 'You're crazy! I mean, Frankie Laine is asking you to supper, Ruby, and you're sitting there and saying no because you're frightened of what your dad will say.' And in a very little voice I said, 'Excuse me, Mr. Laine, may I please come after all?' and he said 'Of course'."

Frankie was travelling with an entourage of about 25, all smartly dressed, and he sat Ruby beside him in the Grand Hotel in Royal Avenue, Belfast, and she thought she must be dreaming.

"They served melon first", she said, "and I didn't know how to eat it, but my mother always said to me that if you don't know what to do watch other people, and I was between him and Carl Fisher, so I watched and I listened, and I suppose I talked a bit too, because he made it so easy."

At 2am Frankie telephoned for a taxi, paid for it, and said to the driver: "Take this lady home." When she arrived the whole street was lit up, and people were out searching for her. Her mother said: "Oh Ruby, your dad's going to kill you. He's that worried." Ruby told her where she'd been, but poor Winnie was too distraught herself to take it in. "Go to bed", she said, "while I find him." The following day Dan took her to the pub with him, something he'd never done before, and said to his mates, without trying to hide the pride in his voice: "Do you know who my daughter had supper with last night? Frankie Laine. Yes, Ruby had supper with Frankie Laine!"

Years later she was in Las Vegas and Frankie was at the Flamingo Club. "I wonder if he remembers", she said. Marie was with her, so she rang his secretary and left Ruby's name. Less than five minutes later he was on the phone to her, saying "Yes, I do remember you coming to supper and I'm glad you made it. I knew you would." He invited them both to supper again after his show at the Flamingo and this time Ruby was able to present herself in something more glamorous than an old twinset and skirt.

But back to the beginning of 1954, when the company came to England with *Yankee Doodle Blarney*, touring first in the provinces and ending at the Metropolitan in Edgware Road.

The Metropolitan was built in 1897, though there had been a theatre on the site since 1836. It was designed by Frank

Matcham, had three floors, gas and electric lighting and heating, and had seating for 2,800. The theatre was modernised in 1908, again by Frank Matcham, and this time it contained tip-up seats and carpeted floors, and went from once nightly to twice nightly. Fred Karno, in whose company such comedians as Charlie Chaplin and Stan Laurel had begun, was top of the opening bill and through the years many famous names passed through the stage door and trod the boards of "The Met", as it was affectionately and familiarly known.

For a while in the Fifties the theatre was advertised as "London's Own Irish Theatre" because so many shows were staged there and Irish performers worked there, and Ruby felt proud to be among them. The Met* was to be a turning point for her, too. It was the night producer Richard Afton saw the show and became excited by this young, exciting, husky-voiced colleen.

Ruby had fallen in love when she was working in a club in Belfast. Jim McGarry (stage name Larry Peters) was a singer who also impersonated Al Jolson. There are so many Jolson imitators, but Larry was very, very good. He was a few years older than Ruby, and she was still unknown.

"I fell in love for the first time, and with a different religion, which was always a hassle with my father being so Proddie. Larry was very handsome and such a happy fellow, and I was so young ... he used to pat me on the head in a sort of 'You're a nice kid' way. I adored him. I used to take our dog for a walk up the street to see his mother, just to catch a glimpse of him. I never grew out of it as my family said I would. Time went on and then we were booked for the same tour and one day he said 'You're grown-up', but still he didn't love me, although he took me out sometimes."

Eventually, Larry left Ireland and went to Canada and Ruby continued with her career, but they always kept in touch. From the Met she sent him a card: "*Yankee Doodle Blarney* going well. Television producer was in tonight; booked me for TV show ..."

When she was 20 Ruby was topping the bill at the London Palladium, and had already made a name with *Softly, Softly, Heartbeat, If Anyone Finds This I Love You, Happy Days and Lonely Nights* and *Let Me Go, Lover.*

"Larry wrote and asked me to marry him. But by then I never knew whether the real attraction was me or the successful singer Ruby Murray. Two different scenes, that's what you've got to sort out. Who loves you for what you are or..."

Larry Peters was killed in a car accident two weeks later and Ruby says now: "I suppose I've loved people after that, but your first love, your first real love..."

**The Met was pulled down in 1963.*

CHAPTER 5

Top of the Pops

Ruby really hit the big time in 1955. Her name was seldom out of the charts or musical papers. When Philip Solomon sold her contract to the Delfont agency in 1954 they, naturally enough, gave her a standard contract, and she couldn't change it.

She shot from earning £15 a week to £100 but says now: "It should have been much more, but that's a lesson you learn. If I had it now I'd probably be on Easy Street, but I'm not unhappy about it because I have what I need and what I want. I don't need a lot in life. No luxury places and big cars. I find I need people more, and I mean real people, not hangers-on. I'm very lucky that I have a lot of good friends."

She stayed with the Delfont agency, with Keith Devon managing her, from 1955 to 1970. By that time they had dispensed with a contract. "They knew I'd give them their percentage without anything written down and, for various reasons, I wasn't doing as much work anyway in the Seventies."

Certainly Ruby didn't splash her money about when she shot into the top bracket. She was working very hard at the recording studios, topping the bill now all over the country, and living in her uncle's house in London.

An illustrated article in *Picture Post* on 23rd April 1955 featured 29 Heiron Street, off Walworth Road, South-East London, part of a row of Victorian terraced houses. It continued: "The room measures about 10ft by 12ft and manages to contain no more than a sideboard, a small upright bookshelf, two armchairs by the open grate, a bare wooden table, a radio and a television set. The flowered wallpaper is faded. An old bull terrier lopes through the room, knocking his legs against the legs of the table. A small, upright window looks out on a grey courtyard. Every morning the postman walks down Heiron Street and deposits a big bundle of letters at number 29.

"For the girl who lives here, who shares this room with her mother and her uncle, is a celebrity. She is perhaps the most successful singer in Britain today. For several months now, three, four, even five of the songs she has recorded have appeared in the list of the week's best-selling discs. She can top the bill at any of Britain's music halls. For her Sunday concerts the halls are packed. She is the star of a television show..."

Ruby had no gramophone, and when a reporter asked her how she listened to her own records she said simply: "Why, on the wireless, of course."

When she and her mother travelled from the north to Bristol they had to change in Birmingham. Ruby had two large, heavy suitcases, and she picked them up, clambered from the train and set off along the platform. Winnie said: "Put them down. *Now walk like a star*. I'll take these. You can't walk like a star with these."

She picked up the cases and hurried off. Ruby made to follow, but an Indian lady alighted from the train, blocking her way, so she waited for her to move off. The woman had with her half-a-dozen bundles, and these she deposited on the platform. Then glancing at Ruby, who had nothing but a handbag to carry, the woman pointed to them.

"She looked like a princess, and wore a beautiful sari and a sparkling jewel on her forehead", Ruby recalled. Ruby picked up the packages, thinking to be helpful and hand them to the Indian woman. But she was already off, almost gliding along...

Hurrying after her, clutching the bundles, Ruby suddenly realised that her mother had gone in the other direction for the Bristol train. She ran after the woman, calling to her, but to no avail; she never even looked round. In desperation Ruby tried to give the bundles to a group of strapping lads coming from the train. "They belong to that Indian lady", she said, "please catch her up with them." They ignored her.

At which point Winnie suddenly reappeared, put the suitcases down, took the bundles from Ruby without a word, and thrust them into the arms of the next batch of Indians coming from the train, saying: "These belong to your crowd." Then she picked up the cases and turned to Ruby: "Come on, follow me. And this time *walk like a star.*"

Lita Roza and Dickie Valentine were among Britain's top singers when Ruby came on the record scene. Coming up with her were Billie Anthony, Ronnie Harris and Ronnie Hilton. When asked the secret of her quick success (quick at least to the paying public) she said: "I suppose it's because I love to sing." The stage fright she suffered in the wings never reasserted itself outside the stage door when thousands of fans were clamouring for her autograph and wanting to speak to her.

"I found it intoxicating. It was magic really", she says. "My father, who had come over to be with me, always made me shake hands with everyone. We did two shows a night and a matinee twice a week. I remember once saying something like not having time today, and he was mad with me. 'They made you' he said, 'and you've always got time for them.'"

In November 1955 thousands of readers of *New Musical Express* voted for their favourite female vocalist. The result was:

Ruby Murray	-	12,687 votes
Alma Cogan	-	11,508 votes
Lita Roza	-	11,445 votes
Joan Regan	-	8,931 votes
Eve Boswell	-	2,200 votes
Edna Savage	-	1,994 votes
Vera Lynn	-	1,272 votes
Billie Anthony	-	1,062 votes
Petula Clark	-	982 votes
Anne Shelton	-	715 votes
Barbara Lyon	-	648 votes
Jill Day	-	607 votes
Patti Lewis	-	577 votes
Marie Benson	-	502 votes
Betty Miller	-	400 votes

Dickie Valentine was the top male singing star with 16,805 votes, his nearest rival being David Whitfield with 9,665. And in the section entitled "Outstanding Popular Singer in the World", Dickie Valentine was fourth and Ruby Murray 13th (from a list of 30, headed by Frank Sinatra). Lita Roza, who was placed third, had been the winner for four years previously.

The hit parade was the all-important list for recording stars. It gave them the power to bargain, pick and choose, and make money. Of course it has to be a good song, and a good singer who can put it over. Even so, through continual repeats, some got through for a while because it is true that, given a reasonable melody and words, a song can "grow on you". You become so used to hearing it that you do eventually like it.

"Plugging" is simply a form of advertising, but the record-spending public left no doubt as to their favourites when it came to buying. They bought 400,000 of Ruby's version of *Softly, Softly* out of the half-million sold. The rest were by various other singers. It worked right through the charts — for instance there were 52 versions of *Stranger In Paradise* and the Eddie Calvert one was the winner.

Many "sensational" new singers were boosted in the Fifties, but a lot dropped by the wayside — making one record, sometimes two, and never being heard of again. Though she toured for years beforehand, Ruby was not heard of in a big way until her television appearance, then everything began to happen to her. This wasn't unique — it happened to Donald Peers also — because added to talent every performer needs a modicum of luck, too.

Ernie Wise recalls seeing Ruby for the first time during a week in variety at the Manchester Hippodrome. "Eric Morecambe and I were on the bill and we all stayed with Mrs. Mackay at 11, Daisy Avenue. They were good digs. Ruby was a hot property after her hit records, Keith Devon was looking after her and I don't think they liked us talking to her. She was a sell-out and I remember thinking I wonder how much they are paying her!"

In fact it wasn't Ruby who was making the money, but quite a few of the other people involved. Although she had been so long in show business, she admits that at 20 "I was utterly green on the business side of things".

Singer Dorothy Squires once told me: "Ruby was exploited, there's no doubt of it. She should have made millions. I admire Ruby tremendously, she has star quality. All the major stars have it and I recognised it the first time I heard her. I had recently returned from Hollywood and was driving home with my then husband, Roger Moore. The car radio was on and during the eight months we had been in the USA Ruby had shot to fame. You don't have to have the greatest voice in the world, but it must have that extra something. Ruby's had. I don't know if it was the huskiness or what, but it was very definitely there."

Frankie Vaughan says the recording business on such levels was quite new then. "Many of us ought to have been making more money, I suppose. I was topping the bill at the London Palladium for £500 a week when the American comedian Danny Kaye was getting £7,000. There was exploitation going on I suppose, but it wasn't anything I was aware of at the time. For me it was simply wonderful to be topping the bill at the Palladium and I'm sure it was the same for her. And looking back, £500 was a fortune then...I don't think anybody understood the long-term value of what was happening."

The *Daily Mirror*'s TV Disc Festival was organised through a nationwide ballot in the paper's columns to choose the stars for the show. The result, in the order in which votes were cast, was Ruby Murray, Alma Cogan, Joan Regan, Dickie Valentine, David Whitfield, Max Bygraves, Eddie Calvert, Ted Heath and his Band, and The Stargazers. The show was televised from the Palladium on 13th November, 1955 and was a huge success.

The *Daily Mirror* ran a "Thank Your Star" competition in conjunction with the event, asking readers to write 500 words or less on "Why I want to say thank you to a recording artiste".

Winners had a five-course lunch with the star of their choice at London's Cafe Royale.

Jean Ryan from Merstham, Surrey, was one of the winners. She had walked into a record shop to buy a Ruby Murray disc. "As I hurried into the cubicle to play it I bumped into a young man. We both fell on the turntable and have been going around together ever since!" The boy was called Bob Jones. Jean was then 16.

Another story that emerged from the event, though it didn't win the lunch, was from a lady in Ilford who wrote that Ruby Murray singing *If Anyone Finds This I Love You,* made her keep her daughter instead of sending her for adoption as she had planned. "Through this", she wrote, "I am now very happy watching her grow into a lovely child".

In Sidcup, Kent, another reader heard Ruby sing this song and as a result obtained permission from an orphanage to invite two little girls home. "And what happiness I have found from this", she wrote.

On the lighter side, Raymond Dodd (then 16) of Brighton was spurred to great heights by Ruby singing *anything*. "As soon as I hear Ruby sing", he wrote, "I feel like doing ten boys' homework!"

She received so many letters that a fan club was formed which continued until 1973. David Frankish ran it from 1965 until 1973 and it kept Ruby in touch with thousands of fans all over the country, previewing recording sessions and stage appearances as well as providing family news and photographs. The combined Christmas/January issue usually gave information about Ruby's summer season because many fans waited until they knew where she'd be before booking their own holiday.

The fan club expanded to other countries also, and in the 1961 *Ruby Murray Fan Club Magazine from Ceylon* Ruby has written: "My secretary has told me what an enthusiastic and loyal lot you are and also a great amount about your activities." These included supper dances, swimming parties, and contributions for various projects, such as the Fatima Hospital Building Fund.

It is interesting to note that even in 1961 the editor was writing about the "problem generation", setting forth in the magazine the contemporary views of some of them.

Ruby's star rose a decade after the war was over — yet so much was still "utility" and "austerity". During the Sixties "the young ones" began to make their presence felt in ways previously denied to parents and grandparents by lack of money, observance of tradition and less advanced education. Ruby and a host of other popular young singers symbolised for many that same "young generation" with at least as many hopes and fears as their ancestors. The editor of her fan magazine wrote: "This magazine dwells on the aspirations of a club which in turn embodies the views and ideas of a young generation. It is our duty to acclaim these ideals. In these times 'teenagers' are considered more elusive than Darwin's 'missing link'. It is up to us to elucidate the basic ideals and thoughts of the so-called 'problem generation.'"

She continued: "To most of us the problem is no problem at all. It may seem therefore that the so-called mature generation has created a problem simply because they do not understand, or fail to comprehend the behaviour of a generation which no doubt craves a more liberal and free existence.

"There is no doubt that the child of today is more precocious than the child of yesteryear. The immense advancement in science, and the fact that today we live in the Atomic Age, gives ample scope for the more dynamic nature of the younger generation.

"Being born into a world devastated by war, the young generation of today has different ideals and a different sense of values. The clue to understanding the modern teenager lies not in a detailed analysis of his or her actions, but by a scrutiny of the circumstances which have made them what they are. Fan clubs have arisen from the added value given by enthusiasts to modern songs and singers. We wonder how many of the so-called abhorrers of modern teenagers would join fan clubs, and general teenage activities, if they had the time and leisure.

"It is not for us of the present to judge which is better, but to pursue enthusiastically our ideals to their legitimate conclusion, believing that our own contribution to the welfare of society is no small one."

Ruby kept closely in touch with fans from all over the world through the club, always reading the newsletters before they were sent out, and signing hundreds of photographs for club members.

Author Michael Thornton collected her records: "I admired her voice, I still do, but apart from this I warmed to her because of her personality. In an era when so many female pop stars were bouncily self-confident Ruby was different; a one-off. She didn't flash wide, bright and artificial smiles like most of the other girl singers. There was a wistfulness in her rather anxious blue eyes, and sometimes a hint of sadness."

For so many, Ruby symbolised the fairy story come true. She was "the girl next door" with added glamour; the ideal daughter who, in spite of great success, stayed close to her family. And she was the girl who made good; if she could do it, so could others. It gave them a dream that one day it could all happen for them, too.

Ruby met Ray Lamar about this time. He was touring manager for Bernard Delfont and was usually about at the weekends, fixing up digs and generally seeing to the well-being of everyone in the company. Ray had been in showbusiness since 1934, when he ran away from home at the age of 16 to become a pierrot with a group called Harry Gold's Yachtsmen who performed on the beach at Ramsgate, Kent.

"We did three shows a day", he said, "and there were 14 changes of programme a week. Between acts we took it in turns to go round with the bottle, persuading the audience to part with their coppers to pay the artistes." Ray was a dancer and saxophonist in those days and when the season at Ramsgate finished he went on the halls, appearing at various times with all the greats of the time.

During the war he was a captain in the Tank Regiment and took part in the D-Day landings. When the war ended he went back into showbusiness on the management side. During his 30-odd years with the Delfonts, Ray managed and toured with many star names. They included Sammy Davis Jnr, Johnnie Ray, Guy Mitchell, Judy Garland, Max Bygraves and Dickie Henderson. Ruby was 18 when they met — but let Ray tell the story himself:

"I worked for the Bernard Delfont Agency and I was assigned to look after Ruby and manage her recording sessions, theatre tours and personal appearances. I was divorced from my first wife and lived alone. We had some great times, even though Ruby was working tremendously hard and the pressure on her time was enormous.

"I met her father Dan and all her family when we played a theatre in Belfast. Dan was a wonderful man, justly proud of his daughter, and we became very good friends. He loved going greyhound racing and I used to go with him. We had a few good winners. Dan seemed to know everybody. He loved company and he liked his drink. We got on well.

"I had a flat in Nell Gwynne House, Sloane Square, London, and Ruby had a flat on the floor above with Marie, her friend from Belfast. I used to take some of the overflow of her family on the numerous visits they made to London. The three of us, Ruby, Marie and myself, had some great times on tour, shielding Ruby from the tremendous pressures of stardom.

"We used to take a boat on the river, go for long country rambles and sit talking far into the night. Gradually I realised I was falling in love with her."

Ruby was unaware of this and went on to become infatuated with first one, then another, young man. "She gets notions", her mother once said. "She gets crushes on people." Sometimes older men featured in her dreams, too.

The only song she fought to sing — and it was another success for her — was *Slowly With Feeling*. That was because she allegedly fell for someone closely connected with the music. "There wasn't an affair", she said, "because he was married at the time and it simply didn't happen. However, I trailed my mother, who was like a third arm in those days, in and out of Boosey and Hawkes (the music publishers) on the slightest pretext. She used to say, 'Oh Ruby, not again'..."

Yet the Press linked Ruby's name with various men during this period and one of them, singer Danny Purchase, caused quite a furore with her father. What happened couldn't have been more innocent. Danny, billed as "The Gypsy Singer", also came from Ireland and he and Ruby were friends and colleagues. While working together on tour they spent an afternoon on the beach in the company of the afore-mentioned Father John Caden, who was a friend of both. Danny, who wanted a little publicity, had previously telephoned the newspapers, and sure enough a couple of photographers arrived and took some pictures.

The following day, photographs of Danny, with his arm round Ruby, appeared in the national Press. There was no sign of Father John, who had been cut from the photographs, and the captions were provocative — "New boyfriend for Ruby", "He's lovely, says singing star Ruby Murray", "Sweethearts on the Beach..." Not for the first time her father demanded to know what was going on. "I don't want to read about your romances in the Press", he said, "especially with a Catholic gypsy who wears an ear-ring." In vain, Ruby protested that there was no romance, that it was simply newspaper talk, but Dan would not be placated.

CHAPTER 6

American dream

Conductor Ray Martin was insistent. "Try to look sexy" he urged, but as Ruby Murray now admits: "I didn't know how to. I'm sitting there trying to visualise how to look sexy for these photographs they're going to take for the sleeve of the record." The result is not the most flattering photograph ever taken of Ruby. "I pushed my bust out and tried to look from underneath my eyelids, but somehow I don't think it worked."

Ruby's sense of humour is one of the great things about her. It helped get her through the bad times, but most of the problems came later. Back in the Fifties time was still golden for the girl they billed as "The Velvet-Voiced Songstress".

Apart for her records, which were selling like the proverbial hot cakes, Ruby was topping the bill in variety shows around the country. In 1955 she went to America on a record promotional tour — no singing, simply touring the States and sounding out the temperature.

She took with her the *Daily Mirror* award which was won by Frank Sinatra in the same poll in which she had gained her own award, and she was enthusiastically looking forward to meeting him when she presented it. But first she had to get past the reporters waiting at the airfield. As she stepped from the plane a battery of cameras was lined up and one of the photographers called out: "Come on, honey! Let's have some cheesecake!"

Norrie Paramor and his wife Joan were with her and Ruby turned to him and whispered: "What do they mean, cheesecake? A smile?" Before he could reply, one of them called out: "Come on, let's see your legs, honey! Lift your skirt!" Ruby recalls: "I became all Irish and thought 'No, I'm a *singer*.'" She adds now, with a chuckle: "Maybe that's why my records don't sell well in the States!" They do well enough in Canada and Australia. But although I went to America four times, and didn't do too badly, I've never had the success there I've had elsewhere."

That first American tour took place when she was almost 21 and, because it was her first time abroad, friends suggested she should buy some luxury clothes and look like a star. "I was always being told to look like a star, 'not an ordinary person'. But I was, and still am, an ordinary person. With a voice that caught the public's imagination, that's true, but as prone to the ills and failings of life as everybody else."

However she went to a furrier in Grosvenor Street and ordered a made-to-measure blue beaver coat. "A magnificent coat it was, too", she said. "Full back and full sleeves, and a lovely pearly blue lining with my name embroidered on the pocket". When she reached the airport Joan and Norrie Paramor were there waiting for her, and Joan was wearing an identical coat — the only difference was the name on the pocket. She had been to the same furrier! They both laughed about it and Ruby said: "We shall be called the Terrible Twins."

One of the highlights of that trip was meeting Frank Sinatra and presenting his award. "He was lovely", Ruby said. "Meeting me didn't mean anything to him, but meeting him meant a lot to me."

Ruby and the Paramors went to Hollywood for the presentation, and were introduced to Sinatra on a recording session. He had done his homework, and knew she was a singer. But this was a promotional trip without concerts, and he said to her: "Gee, I bet you're glad you don't have to sing with a throat like that. What a terrible cold you've got." She didn't tell him she talked that way all the time, because she felt so shy. "I'm sure he couldn't have really been bothered about it."

Joan was chosen as "chaperone" for Ruby who was officially under age. She recalls: "There were many highspots on that trip. We spent a weekend in Las Vegas sightseeing, and went to one of the famous gaming houses, The Golden Nugget. The entrance was adorned with a million dollars in notes and we spent a few cents on the one-armed bandits, then went into the bar, which we later learned had a 'million dollar licence'. We asked for three orange juices, then sat down, and when the waiter brought the drinks he looked at Ruby and asked her how old she was. When she replied that she would be 21 next week, he snatched up the drinks, and screamed at us 'Get out or I'll lose my licence!' Their laws were very strict and Ruby looked very young."

Ruby enjoyed the luxury of having money for the first time in her life. "There was a smell of affluence about the hotel", she said. "It was magnificent and so comfortable. But it was the first time on my own and I badly wanted to share it all with someone. Norrie and Joan were along the corridor, but I needed someone of my own. I looked out on the most wonderful view. Hollywood was all lit up below me, and there I was with two bedrooms, a lounge, bathroom, bar and balcony. My childhood home would have fitted into this one suite easily!"

She loved being able to buy something without counting the cost. Often it wasn't for herself at all, but for her family and friends. "Back home if my mum saw something she admired in a shop window it was wonderful for me to be able to go in and get it for her without even having to ask the price", she said. "After all the years of struggling and saving it was magic."

Her sister Lilian, whom Winnie and Dan had left in Canada with her aunt all those years ago, was now grown-up and married with a small daughter of her own. She had returned to Ireland once, when she was eight, for a brief holiday. But the complete family had not met since.

Lilian lived in Toronto, and during that American trip Ruby telephoned her and arranged to go to Canada for a few days instead of returning with Norrie and Joan. Ruby's memories of her sister were vague. She was only six-years-old when Lilian had been over, and they set about catching up on the lost years.

She met Lilian's friends — "We had a party every night" — and they telephoned Winnie and Dan, though most of the time was used up without talking, only crying. Impulsively, Ruby said: "Come back with me for a while, I'll pay all expenses."

Lilian agreed, but they didn't tell their parents. So when Winnie and Dan arrived at the airport to greet Ruby, almost on the eve of her 21st birthday, out of the plane stepped the daughter they hadn't seen for 17 years — with the two-and-a-half-year-old grand-daughter they had never seen. It was a very emotional Irish reunion. Lilian looks a lot like Ruby, but of course the accent was so different. The photographers took pictures of Winnie hugging her Transatlantic daughter, of Winnie and Dan gazing at their grand-child with tears in their eyes, and of Ruby, a bit dewy-eyed too, standing back and willingly foregoing the limelight on this occasion. She has always maintained that she was the least ambitious of people. "I love singing and I want to sing to the people, but I never desired fame. I didn't ask for it, and I tried my best to cope with it."

Coping with fame wasn't easy for her. She loved the luxury, but she also loved the simple life and often it was difficult marrying the two. Once she was famous she couldn't date a boy she fancied and often he was too nervous to date her. After all she was Ruby Murray, a star; a famous person, someone who was earning more money than he was. Often she likened herself to the Princess who met a charming man in the woods — and didn't tell him she was a princess.

She needed to meet people as people, not as a star versus a fan. At 20 she wanted to be accepted as a young girl; but because of her talent she was pushed into higher echelons. She found it difficult to distinguish between those who wanted to know *her*, and those who wanted to know a *star*.

Back home Joan and Norrie Paramor organised a 21st party for Ruby at their house. Columbia Records supplied a cake and Ruby posed happily for "key of the door" pictures for the Press, and cut up her cake to send to members of her fan club.

Lilian, whose marriage was on the rocks — though Ruby hadn't known that at the time — stayed for several months and travelled with her sister when she next went on tour.

In 1955 Ruby starred with Norman Wisdom in *Painting the Town*, her debut in a musical show. Her mother was with her for the first rehearsal and they were sitting in the Palladium, and Ruby was crying. "It was the combination of several things", she said. "It was a 'cold' theatre, I knew no-one and I was terrified. Every act that came on was so good and I thought 'What am I doing here in the greatest theatre in the world? I want to go home.' I even said to my mother, 'I want to go back and be safe...'"

Practical Winnie, who loved her new life travelling with her famous daughter and meeting so many celebrities and stars, comforted her: "You'll be all right, love. Don't you worry." Ruby went up to sing her song, but not a note came out. It was down to sheer terror because there was no audience, no warmth, and the "tycoons" Bernard Delfont and Val Parnell (who she later came to know, like and respect) were watching out front. She tried again and again, then she heard them shouting and realised that Keith Devon was arguing with Val Parnell. She heard Val say: "I thought you said this girl could sing?" And Keith, all worked up, saying: "Give her a chance, she's frightened."

Swallowing hard, Ruby tried again but when she gets nervous her voice dries up. Yet as a professional she somehow always gets over it. "A whisper came out", she said, "and I worked on it, and suddenly it was all right. Once I settled down it wasn't so bad and I made it in the end."

The Press opening was on a Thursday, and it went well. Friday was the big day, when the public would decide for themselves. It was a magic night. "I could feel the warmth and love of the people coming over the footlights and it was wonderful", said Ruby.

On Saturday her family and friends from Ireland were coming over. The flat in Sloane Square, where she was then living, had one bedroom, a tiny kitchen, bathroom and lounge. All the visitors wanted to stay with her. "Fortunately", she said, "they all drank a lot, except for mummy who had upped her intake from one to two sherries! So they drank until they fell down and slept where they fell!"

She had three shows to do on Saturday, and when she awoke with a sore throat she gargled, took her temperature and decided to rest her voice and let her relatives do all the talking. However, by the time she reached the theatre it was obvious the sore throat wasn't going to disappear and a doctor was sent for. He diagnosed acute tonsillitis and gave her an injection which got her through the matinee and the first house. But her temperature had soared to 103 degrees and a second opinion was sought, with the result that she was told that no way could she do another show.

Yet despite her tears and nervousness there remained a core of gentle stubborness in her heart; she defied the doctors and went on. She knew she could rest on Sunday - if she could find a space among all the people sleeping in her little flat! She was in great pain, although well-dosed, and as her highest note is a great deal lower that a soprano's lowest that helped too. Nevertheless when she finally came off, to a wonderful ovation and a dressing room full of flowers, she was whipped home very quickly. There, yet another doctor sent for an ambulance and Ruby, in a dressing gown and holding her throat, sat on a chair among her friends and relatives who were by this time well into a party.

Her flat was on the sixth floor and at first the ambulancemen couldn't find her in the crowded room. They had brought a wheelchair upstairs with them. "It's my throat that aches, not my feet", she croaked, trying not to laugh at the amazed expressions on their faces. Marie was sitting with her, and they eventually made it down the stairs and into the ambulance. Then her mother and about ten of her relations clambered in too. They went off to the London Clinic with the Irish contingent singing all the way: *If You're Irish, Come into the Parlour...*

Once in bed, with ice-packs on her throat and injections in her bottom, her mother leant across and said, "It was a great night, Ruby. You were a wonderful success and you're in the best place now, so we're going home to continue the party!" She was out of the show for two weeks and Alissande White, grand-daughter of broadcaster and revue artiste Suzette Tarri, took over the role for that period.

Ray Lamar says he remembers so well seeing the news-vendors' headlines on the placards — "Ruby Goes Into Hospital". "I thought then that when national newspapers headline a star with their Christian name only, she is here to stay for a long, long time", he said.

Norman Wisdom recalls: "It was my very first show at the London Palladium. Ruby was smashing and we had lots of laughs. Laughs on-stage come from such small things, and it is endeavouring to control them that hurts your stomach. We had a great time in *Painting the Town*. We did a children's charity matinee, too, and everyone enjoyed it, not only the kids. We also made a record together called *Two Rivers* and although it never reached number one in the charts it sold reasonably well."

Artist Fred Wood wrote to Ruby asking if he might do her portrait. She agreed. Fred painted several of the pop stars during that period, and for his study of Ruby she wore a delicate pink lace-and-net gown and a black silk shawl.

Best frocks... Ruby (right), aged two, with elder sister Lilian.

Piano party... A happy family picture of Ruby with her parents, Dan ("Big Dan") and Winifred, sister Patsy and her husband. An early oil portrait of Ruby hangs on the wall.

Opposite page: *Far left, clowning with Harry Secombe.*

Left, with Irish film star Barry Fitzgerald at the Glasgow Empire.

Below left, young recording star Ruby with her mother.

Right, Ruby meeting Frank Sinatra. Also pictured is orchestra leader and arranger Norrie Paramor.

Below, Irish pop trio the Bachelors (John, Dec and Con) spin a record for Ruby.

Proud parents Dan and Winnie watch over their talented daughter. In 1955 Ruby had five records simultaneously in the Top Twenty.

With her collection of dolls. A publicity shot from the Fifties.

Bernie Burgess, with a portrait of Ruby. The singer with The Jones Boys became Ruby's first husband.

Frankie Vaughan: "I rate Ruby's voice among the best. It's unique, it's beautiful and it's instantly recognisable. And Ruby's a smashing lady!"

Alma Cogan. She and Ruby had their differences, but the tears flowed when she died.

With Frankie Howerd and friend. Ruby (right) starred with the comedian in the 1956 film "A Touch of the Sun".

Below, with Norman Wisdom. They made their musical debut together in "Painting The Town" (1955) at the London Palladium. "We had loads of laughs," he recalls.

Meeting the Queen at the 1955 Royal Variety Show. Crooner Johnnie "Cry" Ray is in the centre.

Leaving a London nursing home in 1955 after being ordered to take a complete rest because of a throat infection.

CHAPTER 7

Royal Variety Show

Two weeks after her unceremonious trip to hospital Ruby was back at the Palladium — paler, thinner, but as enthusiastic as ever. She needed a nurse with her, and various newspapers took up the cry that she was too thin. Were the powers-that-be working her too hard? Were they monitoring what she ate? Was she truly fit now?

Having a nurse in tow added fuel to the fire, but Ruby said she was fine. When she was in her teens she did become pale, but she had masses of energy. The excitement and nervousness she always felt before going on stage probably contributed to her condition, but she was fit as a fiddle and stronger than she looked.

Father John Caden, the priest who Val Doonican had asked to look after her when she was touring several years before, had become a good friend and he sent her malt and vitamins when she was at the Palladium. "Everyone else gets flowers", she said plaintively. "I get cod liver oil and malt." Some of her fans, also concerned with her illness, sent liver, bacon, and sausages to the stage door.

Later, touring with comedy magician Tommy Cooper, she did receive flowers. It was the first night, and she was so nervous that even the bouquet was shaking. The Mayor of Blackpool was sitting in the front row and Tommy asked Ruby in an aside: "Who booked him? Of course you know he's an escapologist. Just watch him get out of those chains!"

Another time an enormous, and very luxurious, arrangement was handed up to her. Tommy, who was next to her in the line-up on stage, whispered: "That's a very well-kept graveyard!" It was always fun, and hard to keep a straight face, when Tommy was in the show. The two got on very well.

Another artiste who could always make her laugh when she shouldn't was Harry Secombe. "He's a very honest human being", she says, "very kind, and exactly the same off-stage as he is on." In the finale of one show she did with him they had to sing *If You Were The Only Girl in the World* as a duet, but Harry was never able to be serious for more than a few seconds and he'd look at her and make funny faces while she tried to sing seriously. When she and the late comedian Harry Worth were touring together they played tag when the curtain came down, always making sure they were back in their respective places if it rose again for another call.

The nurse stayed with Ruby for a month after her bout of tonsillitis and the two became friends. Ruby always insisted there was no cause for alarm in her condition. When she was nervous or excited, or both, her throat dried up, and she became pale and lost weight; but she soon had the situation under control.

In November 1955 she was listed as one of the artistes for the Royal Variety Show. Ruby was, and still is, extremely proud of the honour. She was also nervous. To calm herself she asked the doctor if he could give her anything so she would be "all right on the night", and he prescribed a blue capsule.

"That will take care of it, don't worry", he said. Reassured, Ruby went to the rehearsals. She forgot to take the pill, and only found it three weeks later! But her performance at the Royal Variety Show was a great success.

She sang some of her record hits and, for an encore, *Dear Old Donegal.* Afterwards she met the Royal Family (most of whom were there) and the Queen asked her if she was enjoying playing the Palladium, and Princess Margaret asked: "Were we a very tough audience?"

But the one she got into a real muddle with was Prince Philip when he said: "You were the wrong side of the border tonight, with Donegal, weren't you?" Ruby admits her geography isn't good, and she answered: "No sir, I come from Northern Ireland.". Now she adds: "I think he was glad to move on!"

Painting The Town ran for seven months at the Palladium, then Ruby went on tour, topping the bill in variety. She was still having trouble getting from the wings to the microphone, and the papers were still commenting on her lack of stage expertise. Most of it was nerves, not inexperience, because Ruby had been singing on stage for a lot longer than many of her critics realised.

What she didn't have under control was her love life. Ruby wanted to fall in love again — and often did, deeply and romantically — but her mother still called these passions "Ruby's notions".

"I think I was looking for a knight in shining armour", Ruby says now, "and it took me a long while to find out there wasn't any such person. I've always been a dreamer, and maybe when I was young even more so."

She went with the CSE (Combined Services Entertainment) to sing for the troops, and enjoyed doing this very much. "It was like going back to the old touring days", she said, "because there was no proper stage, it was all makeshift. We carried our own sound and had our own plane. Derek Agutter (father of actress Jenny Agutter) was in charge and we flew from Brize Norton."

Ruby went to Malta, Aden and Cyprus where her brother Jack was stationed. When she played his camp he said he felt really proud. "I basked in the reflected glory of her fame. To think this glamorous woman on stage was my little sister. It was great. It was also funny to find how many 'brothers' Ruby had." Because the word had been passed around that she had a brother in the forces Jack met several soldiers and sailors who were introduced as "Ruby Murray's brother". But as her real brother Jack did a good trade in autographs and signed photos. Ruby sang everywhere, from the tops of tanks covered in tarpaulin, on board little trawlers, to troops on the embankment. That was in Tobruk.

The other side of the coin were the hospital visits. Ruby recalls one particular visit when she saw someone who had been working with oil and been badly burned. "I'm stupid and squeamish over things like that", she says, "but I was supposed to look at him and ask 'How are you feeling?' Well, he must have been feeling terrible, it was so inadequate. How *could* I say that? I sang in the wards, and did my best, but you come out feeling you've nothing to moan about, that you shouldn't have a care in the world, and wishing, oh wishing so much, that you could do something more to really help."

The first troop concert was to Malta in 1956 and it was there Ruby met Jack Creighton. When she left they agreed to write to each other, and when he came on leave they went about together. Inevitably the newspapers took up the story and made a great romance of it, and Ruby, who was so very fond of Jack, but was not sure if she loved him, went to meet his family. She clicked immediately, especially with his mother, and they are still friends today, "She's such a lovely, gentle person, and we are on the same wavelength", she says.

Jack was a doctor and hailed from Scotland and this time her father had no axe to grind about his religion, for he was a Presbyterian. Yet Ruby wasn't sure when Jack asked her to marry him. She knew she *had* to sing; ambition hadn't a lot to do with it. But the need to sing and mix with stage folk, was very strong and she recognised and acknowledged the fact. How would marriage to a doctor work out? And did she love him enough for marriage? They continued to see each other when they could, which wasn't often because of his RAF career and her showbusiness commitments.

She was touring with Marie as her secretary companion, and travelling everywhere by train when, one day in Worcester, they walked past a car showroom. A Vauxhall Victor was in the window and Marie said: "You ought to have a car, Ruby. You can afford one now and it would be more convenient than the train with all the luggage."

Ruby stopped and thought about the idea for a moment, then looked again at the Vauxhall Victor in the window. "Let's go in and see", she said, asking the astonished saleroom assistant: "Would you mind if we sat in that car, just to get the feel of it?"

Ruby, described so many times as "the girl next door" was seldom recognised. Both she and Marie sat in the car and enthused to each other while the assistant went about his other business. Ruby loved the smell of the new leather, and acknowledged how useful a vehicle would be to them, so when they clambered out she walked over to him and said, "It's beautiful, I'll take it."

He said, "What do you mean, you'll take it?"

"I'll buy it."

"You can't buy that", he said. "It's just come on the market and there's a six months waiting list for it."

Crestfallen, Ruby turned away: "Oh, no use then, I'm only here till Saturday." He was interested, as well as amazed, now. "Where?" he asked, and Ruby told him: "I'm at the theatre. I'm Ruby Murray."

The deal was done and on Saturday, when they finished the show, the Vauxhall Victor was in the car park, all papers completed. There was only one problem. Neither Ruby nor Marie could drive. They both had licences, because in Belfast in those days you didn't need to pass a test to get a licence, and a long time beforehand Marie had suggested it would be a good idea to have them. She always was the sensible one, Ruby says.

"We sent wee Jimmy next door down with ten shillings for two licences. They were five shillings and a small passport photo each. And of course you could use those licences in England, too, always provided you could drive, which neither of us could!"

Ruby did learn later and became a very good driver. She used her Irish licence until it ran out, then she had to pass the test and get herself an English one.

None of that helped now, with a brand new car in the theatre car park and she and Marie due in the next theatre on the Monday. Ruby rang Ray Lamar, her touring manager, and he caught a train to Worcester and drove the shining Vauxhall

Victor to London where he garaged it for her until she had learned to drive it.

Marie, who was married by this time, said her husband Frank would teach Ruby to drive, but Arthur Helliwell, the famous newspaper columnist, heard that Ruby Murray had a new Vauxhall Victor and thought it would make interesting reading. He rang to ask for an interview about the new car.

The afternoon went well until Arthur asked her to take him for a ride and she hesitated, saying the car really still controlled her. He persisted, and in vain she told him she "wasn't really that good yet and it would be better to wait until she was more proficient". But Arthur wanted fodder for his column, and he thought she was simply being ultra-modest, so after a 15-minute verbal fight, she agreed to go round Regents Park with him and her press agent Al Hunt.

Al got in the back and Arthur Helliwell took the front passenger seat. Nervously Ruby took her place at the wheel. She started off with a series of kangaroo jumps. "I managed to get round and back to the flat without actually killing anyone", she said, "although I went over one or two pedestrian crossings where the people jumped smartly out of the way." She invited him up for a cup of tea, saying: "I did tell you I haven't quite mastered the art of driving yet." Both Arthur and Al refused the tea, Arthur saying he needed to walk for a while. Both were ashen-faced when they alighted from the car, and visibly shaking. That Sunday, in his column in the *People* newspaper, Arthur went to town with the headline, "Stock Car Racing round Regents Park with Ruby Murray".

CHAPTER 8

Wedding Belle

Ruby is a great film fan, and when she was touring she spent the afternoons, when there wasn't a show, at the pictures. These days she enjoys delving into the history of the town she is in, but then she liked the escape of the cinema. Especially the romantic films.

She was in a film released early in 1956 called *It's Great To Be Young*. She wasn't seen in the film but her voice was heard singing the theme song *You Are My First Love*. Her other two films were a documentary for Pathé News about how a record is made and, again in 1956, a film starring Frankie Howerd called *A Touch Of The Sun*. Ruby played an Irish chambermaid, and sang two songs, *O' Malley's Tango* and *In Love.*

Dennis Price and Richard Wattis were also in the film, and although her part only took two weeks to film, she met them all and enjoyed being part of the film making. "It seems disjointed while you're doing it", she said, "but it all comes together in the cutting room." There was some talk then of Ruby and Dickie Valentine starring together in a film to be called *The Louder They Sing*, and producer Raymond Stross took a three months option on Ruby's contract, but that film was never made.

At the same time she was in the show at the Brighton Hippodrome. "For the two weeks of filming I was up at 4.30am. The car taking me to the studios at Nettlefold arrived at five, and I had to be made up and on the set by 8.30am."

The Hippodrome show, which also starred Reg Dixon (who had equal billing with Ruby) was twice nightly. The final performance finished about 11pm and there wasn't much time for socialising.

In May, Prince Rainier of Monaco married Grace Kelly, a

Hollywood actress. She also had Irish connections and that fairytale romance and wedding was watched avidly by many romantic young girls in Britain, who had known nothing but austerity all their lives. Things, material things, were just beginning to be easier.

Ray Lamar, road manager for the Delfont agency, asked Ruby to marry him. She liked him enormously but had not thought of him in a romantic context then, and in any case she was still looking for her dream lover. She went out with Ray often, as she did with various other suitors, but maybe she was trying too hard to fit them into her image of a Prince Charming. She said: "Let me do the summer season in Blackpool. It will be good for us to be away from each other for two or three months."

Ray agreed. "It seemed to make sense. We had been together constantly, and the break would help us to be absolutely sure. I couldn't go to Blackpool with her because my duties with other stars would be taking me around most of the rest of the country during the summer."

Ruby had learned to dance while in the Palladium show with Norman Wisdom, and had been teamed with Tommy Steele for a dance number in his television spectacular *The Golden Year*, which celebrated Tommy's wonderful year of 1956. Ernest Maxim, who was producing the summer season in Blackpool for Bernard Delfont, wanted Ruby to include some dancing as well as singing. Because she had not been trained as a dancer, and because she always under-estimates herself, she worried about whether she could do it without tripping or falling over. Most of her spare time then was spent practising.

Bernard Delfont's first summer season in Blackpool was 1957 and he had a great show lined up. Topping the bill with Ruby was Tommy Cooper; comic Ken Platt was a little further down the bill with The Jones Boys, four lads who were doing very well with the harmony group they had formed. Their signature tune was *The Whole Town's Talking About The Jones*

Boys. They had recorded for Columbia and Decca, and had successfully toured since their formation.

Bernie Burgess began in showbusiness at the age of 12 at the New Theatre, Northampton, where his father Leonard Burgess was electrician. He did all sorts of things in the theatre before singing, including being stage manager. He became one of The Jones Boys almost by accident. He went with a friend to an audition for a vocal group to be called the Mell-O-Macs. While there he also auditioned; and it was Bernie, not his friend, who secured the job.

The group worked on their act for a month, rehearsed, revised, rehearsed again then changed the name to The Jones Boys and went on tour, winning fans in every town. That summer of 1957 was their first summer season, too, and it proved very important to them.

Ruby met Bernard Burgess in that show. "He always seemed to be on his own", she said, "and spent a lot of time fishing off the end of the pier. We used to chat, and he was quiet and sad in a way. I always fell in love with sad people, I think. His mother had recently died and we talked about it. I began to look forward to the time we spent together when we came out of rehearsals. He took me out to supper after the show one night, and it went on from there. One day I realised I loved him."

Ruby was on cloud nine and, as impetuous as ever, telephoned her parents to tell them she had met the man she wanted to marry. Dan said they would come over and meet him, and forbade her to make any move until then. Ruby was 22 and Bernie 28. Ruby immediately wrote to Jack Creighton so he wouldn't read of her romance in the newspapers. "I was fond of Jack. I loved him, I suppose, but I wasn't 'in love' with him", she said. "I wouldn't accept his ring. I suppose I knew that his career and mine wouldn't mix, and that we were both dedicated to our careers. I needed to marry someone in showbusiness, but more than anything it had to be someone I loved."

Winnie and Dan arrived in Blackpool to meet Bernie. It was instant war. Both of them had hoped she would marry Jack, and perhaps they were also a little scared that Bernie would take over from them. The feelings were mutual and Ruby, who desperately wanted everyone to get on well together, tried to placate them all. Her parents said: "Wait, you haven't known him long enough", so she and Bernie talked the matter over. They knew her parents would never come round so they decided to marry first and tell them afterwards.

The only people in on the secret were the other members of The Jones Boys, who attended the wedding with their respective girl friends, and the theatre padre, the Rev. Alcock, who conducted the service at Blackpool's Whitegate Baptist Church. The happy couple phoned her parents after the ceremony, before they heard of it through outside sources. That sort of thing is hurtful enough anyway — but if you are in the public eye and the media become involved then it enhances it a hundredfold.

As it was, reporters sought out Jack Creighton and his family and talked to Dan and Winnie, who stoically refused to say too much — though Winnie couldn't resist one remark: "I hope we are not going to be pushed into the background and forgotten." Dan simply said: "This is quite a shock."

Ruby wore a black velvet suit and tiny velvet hat for her wedding, and was quoted as saying: "Bernie is everything I ever wanted. Life for me now is all pink and feathers." They did the show that night, and afterwards cut a huge wedding cake and opened a dozen bottles of champagne for the cast. They had known each other exactly six weeks.

Dan Murray still held on to a dream that the couple could return to Ireland and be married "properly" at Richview Presbyterian Church where Ruby had sung in the choir when she was a small girl. But it wasn't possible because their's had been a church service and not a civil ceremony. Over his shock by now, Dan told Ruby: "Well, you've made your bed..."

Ray Lamar was shattered. "My world fell apart", he said, "Deep in my heart I'd hoped Ruby would say yes to me at the end of the summer. I immersed myself in my work and we did not meet again for 15 years."

Ruby and Bernie announced their engagement on 13th August and were married on the 23rd. At the end of the season they went to Paris for a belated honeymoon, then set about looking for a permanent home. Ruby hoped, and often prayed, that her parents and Bernie would eventually come together.

"I kept thinking that when we had children Bernie would get to like my folks and they would get to like him, but of course it never happened. It just got worse and worse, and I was always in the middle of it."

That Christmas both Ruby and Bernie were booked for pantomimes, Ruby in *Babes In The Wood* at The Liverpool Empire, where Jewel and Warriss were starring, and Bernie in Birmingham. For Ruby it was her first pantomime role — she played Maid Marian, not a large part, but she enjoyed the atmosphere of pantomime very much. Lynette Rae, who later married Val Doonican, was Principal Boy, and the two girls shared digs for a while. Then Ruby and Bernie decided to rent a place to which they could both travel when they had finished work and as each of the trains come into the very famous change-over junction at Crewe, Cheshire, they found a flat over a dress shop there for the pantomime season. "But it was miserable travelling down on my own, and as Bernie's train from Birmingham always arrived after mine I made friends with the porters there. I used to sit with them, drinking tea and swopping stories until he came."

Legendary Principal Boy Dorothy Ward was also in Liverpool in 1956/57. She was in *Dick Whittington* at the Pavilion, and an enterprising reporter asked her what she thought of her "opposition" — the two current pop stars who were appearing in their first pantos — Tommy Steele at The Royal Court, and Ruby Murray at the Empire. "Opposition?" barked Dorothy. "They're not opposition, just kiddies."

The permanent home had to wait a while longer because when the pantomime season was over Ruby was booked to go to America again to appear in the Patti Page show, *The Big Record*, on television. But Ruby said the booking was wrong from the beginning. "It was about as sensible as putting Joan Regan and myself in the same spot at that time, because we did the same type of thing and there is usually only room for one." However, Ruby was booked for the show, and agent Keith Devon told her: "The money's good. Do your best and hope for the best."

She was to sing three songs on *The Big Record* but when she arrived she found her act had been cut to three choruses of *Galway Bay*, which took about 15 seconds and gave her no time to establish any kind of bond with the watching public. After her solo spot, she was in a sketch with Patti Page where she played her wicked stepmother.

"I was in a long grey suit covered in spangles, and had to wear a harsh grey wig with a bun attached, and join in a rock number which I didn't know and wasn't given a chance to prepare. Patti, of course, looked gorgeous. She was Cinderella..."

The New Musical Express printed a headline saying, "Ruby Murray Wins Acclaim on US TV", which Ruby said was a kind thing to do, and helped her feel better in public, but she admitted to herself what a failure the whole thing had been. "However, by then I had got over my tendency to cry when things went wrong, except for a wee weep when I was alone maybe. I tried to think instead, well that's that, and put it down to experience."

She returned from America and went into the summer show at Great Yarmouth, again starring with comedy magician Tommy Cooper. The Jones Boys were also booked, and this was to be their last season together. They were at the Wellington Theatre on the end of the pier and it had a glass roof and guttering. The summer of 1958 produced some violent thunderstorms, and one night while she was singing *How Deep Is The Ocean*, which was extremely popular then, there was a great crash and water began pouring into the theatre. The roof and guttering had gone. "For a few moments there I thought we might be about to find out how deep it was", she said.

She kept on singing, even while people were hurrying towards the exits. "I could hear them backstage calling the chorus girls for the finale so I carried on, cutting bits of the act to reach the end quickly. By then everything was set for the finale, and we all crowded on stage to sing God Save the Queen" — "And us all", some wag muttered during the rendering.

At a party later that week they found out that Anne Hart, who was appearing at the Britannia Pier, had been singing *The Clouds Will Soon Roll By*, while Joan Turner at the Windmill Theatre had been giving vent to *One Fine Day* from "Madame Butterfly".

Ruby had a letter from the management praising her actions in carrying on and avoiding a panic, "I didn't think my act was that bad", she laughed, and the guttering and roof were patched up in time for the show the following night.

Theatre historian Alan Goode was also in Great Yarmouth that year. "It was a long, hot summer", he remembers, "and I was a barker with one of the two sideshows on the pleasure beach. Standing side-by-side was The Smallest Living Pixie and Victor/Victoria, the living half-man and half-woman. I never met Ruby until almost the closing week of that season, but Tommy Cooper I came to know very well.

"He called in at our show most evenings on his way to the Wellington Pier, and he always seemed to time his arrival to coincide with the moment when I was giving my histrionic all! This followed a familiar pattern... 'Inside these plain, sealed envelopes, Victor/Victoria answers those questions which I know you are aching to ask. But I beg you, ladies and gentlemen, with the deepest sincerity, that if you purchase one of these envelopes will you please, please, please, take care that on no account do the contents fall into the hands of very young people. Thank you very much indeed.'

"The envelopes were on sale at sixpence each, and Tommy Cooper's vast face always seemed to suddenly loom over all the other heads in front of me just as I reached my dramatic bit, 'and I beg you with the deepest sincerity...' and I would dissolve into helpless, hysterical laughter, and we sold no envelopes at that performance."

On Mayor's Day all the stars appearing in the resort spent the day at the pleasure beach, working in turn on the stalls, the rides and sideshows. All the money taken went to the Mayor's Fund to help a charity of his choice. That was when Alan Goode finally met Ruby. He did an act of walking barefoot through fire. The TV cameras recorded it and Ruby was there to kiss the brave (or foolhardy) soul who had risked it.

During that season comedian Stan Stennett, who was appearing on the other pier, took Ruby up in his light aircraft. "Stan is an expert pilot but even so I was scared", Ruby admitted. "The plane was so small and it didn't help either when Anne (Anne Hart) said to me jokingly: 'You're not going up in *that*, are you? He knitted it himself!' Luckily we didn't have another storm that afternoon and I really enjoyed it, though I have to admit that I gave a huge sigh of relief when we were on terra firma again, which made Stan laugh."

For that season Ruby and Bernie rented a cottage just outside Yarmouth; but when Winnie came to see them he refused to let her stay with them and she booked into a hotel, which added fuel to the already explosive parent/daughter/husband situation.

Winnie and Dan had separated by then, to Ruby's great regret. "I suppose I wanted everything nice and cosy, but life isn't always like that, I know. In any case Dan never visited when Bernie was about."

CHAPTER 9

The Singing Mum

After the Great Yarmouth season Ruby and Bernie bought a bungalow in Oxshott, Surrey, and discussed their future. The Jones Boys had had an offer from Australia, but Ruby didn't want to go because she really does like to be either in England or Ireland. The Australian contract was for a long tour, and neither of them wanted to be absent for too many months. Ruby was also doing very well in Variety, and although she hadn't had a hit in the charts for some while, it seemed foolish to miss this opportunity when, as she well knew, it might not come again.

Show business is a mercurial profession, and while Ruby was popular she wanted the chance to work. Thirty years on and she is still popular and working, but she wasn't to know that would be so then. Bernie wasn't keen to go because, although they had been married almost two years, they were just buying a house, and he was thinking of going into the management side of showbusiness. So The Jones Boys went off without Bernie, and Ruby carried on in Variety in Britain.

Their new home in Surrey was featured in numerous magazine articles, and Ruby was pictured dusting or washing up, and the captions spoke of married bliss and domesticity. But after a few months the real picture was slightly different.

"Not Bernie's fault, maybe not mine either", Ruby says now. "We were such different people in our outlook." Bernie was a disciplinarian and Ruby found it hard to understand why it mattered so much that they kept silent at mealtimes and that everything had to be so strictly right. Life, for her, didn't fall into set patterns and you couldn't make it do so. Bernie is a very organised person, and at that time the other important thing was that Ruby was earning the big money. "You have to be a very special person to stand back and listen to somebody else taking all the glory", Ruby said, "Bernie was never happy doing that, because he wanted to be on his own. That was very understandable but it was not good for the sort of situation we were in."

She had always been close to her family and once she was earning she sent them money each week. When they married Bernie thought it ought to stop. "You can't go on doing it forever", he said, "because you won't be able to keep it up, and you're married now. They shouldn't expect it."

It created a lot of hassle. Dan was angry with Ruby, not because of the loss of the money, though it meant he could not now treat everyone in the pub — which he loved to do — but mostly because she was listening to Bernie.

Ruby used to say, "Well, he *is* my husband"; and then she'd fight with Bernie over it and say, "Well, they *are* my parents." It added to the stress, and all Ruby wanted was for everyone to be happy. "I'd have given them anything if only they could all have got along together, but they didn't, and you can't make people like each other, I know that now", said Ruby.

In 1959 Bernie went with Ruby on her second American tour. "It wasn't too bad until we reached Chicago", she said. She was booked for a spot in the Keyman's Club there and was rehearsing her opening number, *It's A Great Day For The Irish,* when the owner came in.

"We don't want that stuff", he said, "We want Irish songs."

"Well, it says it's a great day for the Irish. It's hardly Jewish", she told him, in an attempt to appear lighthearted.

It transpired that they wanted rebel songs, and Ruby refused. "I was booked to sing Irish songs, and *this* is the sort of Irish song I sing", she said, implying "take it or leave it".

The manager got his own back in his introduction, "We've got a girl here", he said, "we've brought her all the way from Ireland, and we're paying her a *fabulous* sum of money, her fare and her husband's fare and their hotel bill. By the way, she's from Belfast."

The audience turned their backs — most of them were loyal American Dubliners — and many went to the bar and ignored her. But Ruby stuck it out and did the 30 minutes she had to do. "It nearly killed me", she said, "but I wouldn't give in." She came off and burst into tears in front of Bernie, who went to the manager and said: "How dare you treat my wife like this!" The ensuing argument led to a fight.

The manager did apologise to both of them — maybe because he could see they weren't intimidated — and he admired Ruby's stand not to sing rebel songs but to stick to her programme, whatever the provocation.

Ruby was worried about the tax situation between America and England because the manager of the club had not exaggerated the money she was being paid — it was good. She spoke to the tour manager, an Irishman, who said: "Nothing to worry over. Meet me tomorrow and we'll get it sorted out."

The following day he took her to the Tax Officer and said: "Hullo, Mike. I've got this little girl from the old country to do a few gigs and of course I'm paying her in dollars. Would you stamp this to clear her for going home when the tour's finished?"

Mike looked up and smiled at her. "Sure, no problem. Have a good trip", he said, and Ruby came out wondering why she worried so much.

Perhaps, she thought, it's to do with my condition, for by now she was expecting her first child. However, she was also booked for another troop tour and went with Bernie to Malta, Cyprus and Tripoli. It was in Cyprus that she left her trousers behind. She had put two pairs under the mattress to keep them smart — then forgot to pack them. On the plane going home she remembered and a frantic telephone call went out to brother Jack from the airport when they touched down. "Please retrieve my trousers from hotel so and so, room so and so..."

"One day she'll forget herself, so she will", was Jack's answer, but he nevertheless rescued and posted the trousers to her.

Her latest recording success — *Goodbye, Jimmy, Goodbye*, in memory of her Uncle Jimmy, who had been killed at Dunkirk — had been in the charts for some time and the soldiers requested it at every show. She would have included it anyway, because it was the latest; but it had a special meaning for many of them, even if they weren't named Jimmy.

When they returned, Ruby went into rehearsals for a pantomime in Manchester — *Dick Whittington*. Freddie Mills was playing Idle Jack; it was his first pantomime and he was very nervous. His favourite story, he told Ruby, was about a little Irishman who'd had too much to drink and had been thrown out of a flat several storeys high. He was mad about this and was shouting at the top of his voice, and from the safe distance of the ground: "I'm not afraid of youse! Come down and fight Paddy O'Murphy!"

Freddie Mills lived in the same block of flats and was walking by at that moment. He stopped to see what the commotion was and Paddy, recognising him, quickly linked arms and started shouting up to the window: "Come down, the lot of youse, and fight Paddy O'Murphy and Freddie Mills!"

Ruby planned to have her baby in Bernie's home town, Northampton, because when they lived there at the beginning of their marriage she had grown to like and trust the gynaecologist, Dr. Watson, who was Irish himself.

The pantomime went well, with Ruby letting out the laces in her dress (she played Fat Alice Fitzwarren) just a little bit more each day. When the panto season finished she planned a complete rest at her in-laws (Bernie's father and his sister lived close) until the great day. However, she wasn't too well and when the hospital doctors checked they found her blood was in danger of clotting, and decided to admit her and keep tabs on her progress. Although she thought it unnecessary, Ruby acquiesced with good grace and spent the waiting for baby time in hospital — either reading, writing or knitting.

Dr. Watson performed a caesarean on 5th May, 1960, and when Ruby regained consciousness they placed her daughter in her arms. "She had a mass of red hair and a terribly yellow skin because she was jaundiced", Ruby said, "but she was so beautiful."

The baby was christened Julie Amanda at the church in Blackpool where Ruby and Bernie had been married. She was four weeks old then and Ruby was in the summer show at the Palace with Harry Secombe and Harry Worth. Bernie went, too, and they rented a house and had a happy time. But trouble started again when Winnie came to visit. Bernie, reasonably enough, didn't want the baby spoiled, and when any of the family picked her up and cuddled her, he protested. Ruby wanted to hold her as much as possible; she is a very demonstrative person. But Bernie had strong views over the way a child should be brought up. Continual nursing and fussing was, in his eyes, bad.

Julie became a much travelled baby, touring Ireland with them at six months old, when Ruby again played many of the tiny country places she knew from way back. To add to the nostalgia, Marie joined them, accompanying Ruby on the piano, "so it was almost like old times". It was a happy trip, followed soon afterwards by a grand tour of South Africa with Paul and Sally Burnet. Paul Burnet had been the musical director for The Jones Boys, and had become a personal friend to Ruby and Bernie. They all sailed on the *Pendennis Castle.*

It was Ruby's first trip on a big liner, and she enjoyed it very much. Just over two weeks after leaving Southampton they arrived in Capetown. "I'll never forget my first view of Table Mountain and all the lights from the houses below twinkling and looking so pretty", she said.

Their timing was right, too, for it was St. Patrick's Day and also the day South Africa left the Commonwealth, and the flags and bunting were out. They disembarked to a band playing rousing tunes, and a bevy of officials waiting "obviously for someone important", Ruby remarked to Bernie. They soon discovered it was for them, and they rode in an open car through the streets which were lined with what they hoped were their potential audiences. Certainly they were given a royal welcome and Ruby was surprised at the really great popularity of her records over there.

They toured Capetown, Durban and Johannesburg and played to packed theatres and enthusiastic audiences. They also found time for some sightseeing and rode to the top of Table Mountain in a cable car, "a nerve-racking but wonderfully exhilarating experience".

When they returned Ruby appeared in an edition of *Sunday Night at the London Palladium* and won good reviews from most of the critics.

Rock 'n' roll made a great dent in the careers of the recording artistes when it first hit Britain in the Sixties. Those who survived the onslaught went on for a few more years, but were overtaken in the charts by the new sounds. Ruby was hurt by the premature listing of her name among the stars of yesteryear, "because although I was no longer in the charts and seldom on television I was working all the time in Variety".

Rock 'n' roll had really started in the mid-Fifties. Bill Haley had a hit with *Shake, Rattle and Roll* in December 1954, and another with *Rock Around the Clock* in the spring of 1955, but it wasn't until the film *The Blackboard Jungle* was released in November 1955 that it really got under way. The re-issued *Rock Around the Clock* topped the charts in November and there was no looking back. In the spring of 1956 Elvis Presley was into *Heartbreak Hotel*, and, although for a while the ballad singers and the rock 'n' rollers ran together, by the Sixties rock was on top.

Ruby and Bernie employed a nanny, Jane, who went on tour with Ruby until Julie was old enough for school. It was Jane's first job, and her first time away from home, so she was naturally a little apprehensive.

"But it was marvellous, really. Right from the start I was treated as one of the family rather than as an employee, and I loved it all."

CHAPTER 10

Joys of Touring

Ruby and Bernie had started the company Ruby Murray Enterprises when they married; but apart from the fact that both of them were directors, they had nothing to do with the day-to-day running of the business side of it. They left that to the people concerned, the solicitor and accountant Ruby had employed when she first started to earn big money.

"I had no business experience and I confess I wasn't really interested. I simply wanted to sing, and I was happy enough to sign the cheques and believe, naively perhaps, everything I was told."

Since 1954/1955 Ruby's earnings had reached the highest income tax rate. She had spent freely, buying a house for her parents, various businesses for her brother and cars for the rest of the family. She is a modest person regarding money, not feeling the need for status symbols; her criteria when she bought anything was how much comfort or pleasure it would give, never going for the highest price in a snobbish sort of way. And in spite of two years outside the charts, which the critics made much of, she was doing very nicely with her records and her variety act. She trusted the accountant and solicitor and therefore it was a double shock when she picked up an envelope from the mat one morning in 1960, slit it open and read that if she did not pay £17,000 income tax within seven days she would be taken to court.

It was one of the biggest traumas she had to face. "I hadn't got anything like that amount of money", she said. "We had the house, car, and life insurance. Of course I nearly died, because my second biggest worry is debt. I have to know that I don't owe people. I like to pay as I go along."

They discovered that neither the accountant nor the solicitor were keeping books, and that the two of them had "really done me over." Both were put out of business through it, but as Ruby said: "At the time it didn't do me a lot of good." She wasn't the only one to be caught, but that didn't help either. It all came at a time when her earnings were nothing like as high as they had previously been.

She and Bernie decided to sell the house, which they both loved, and buy a smaller one. The same tactics were employed with the car, although, as Ruby said at the time, it wasn't an outrageous one anyway, and she needed a vehicle, however small, for getting to work. They cashed in their life insurances but still it left them £8,000 short of the required amount.

The only answer was to work as hard as possible until it was paid off, which is what Ruby set about doing. They bought the 17th century Rectory Cottage at Wootton, near Northampton, where Bernie came from. The property was smaller and run-down, but included a quarter of an acre for them to build a centrally-heated extension. In total it cost £4,000 — £2,000 for the property and £2,000 for refurbishing. They bought it with a mortgage, which, as soon as she had enough money, Ruby paid off.

Al Hunt, who had been her publicity agent, died and she was now with his assistant, Brian O'Hanlan. But Brian wanted to concentrate more on legitimate theatre, so they parted by mutual consent. Author and theatre reviewer Eric Braun and his partner, Anna Matthews, took on the job.

Ruby and Bernie went to meet Eric at a large block of flats near Marble Arch, London, which included Anna's flat and the headquarters of their agency. Ruby said: "As we were crossing the courtyard a green sports bike cut in front of us. The owner parked it against a wall, clicked a lock shut and whipped off his cycle clips. 'Miss Murray, Mr. Burgess, I'm Eric Braun', he said, 'Come'. Before we could quite recover from our surprise he ushered us into a lift and up to Anna's flat. In the course of conversation we learned that he went everywhere by push-bike, and this was the method he would use to cover our tours and advance publicity."

Eric recalled: "It was 1962 when the late C.W. (Jack) Ingham, one of the warmest of Fleet Street's show business writers, phoned me to say that Ruby Murray and her husband, Bernard Burgess, were looking for a new publicity agent. At first I was a little doubtful that my late partner Anna Matthews and I could legitimately take on another client. We had so many. Could we find the time to give sufficient care and attention to a lady who was at the very top of the tree in the recording industry?

"Bernie and Ruby came to see us in the block of flats in Edgware Road where we had an office. They came, we saw, and we were completely conquered by their warmth and sincerity and, above all, the utterly unassuming manner of their approach; it was as if they were doing us a favour by coming to see us.

"Tin Pan Alley, as it was then called, was a tough hurly-burly, but none of this seemed to have rubbed off on Bernie and Ruby, particularly Ruby, whose gentleness explained in a flash why her top hit had been *Softly, Softly*. It was tailor-made for her and unthinkable for any other girl singer, then or now.

"I fell, hook, line and sinker. Anna and I agreed that the Burgesses would be in my special domain. The arrangement was that Anna and her assistant would, as we laughingly said, 'Hold down the London desk', while I handled the advance touring side of the business by bike. In Ruby's case there was likely to be a great deal of this. After seeing to advance publicity, and cycling up again for the opening and closing nights for Ruby and Bernie's summer season in Margate with Hughie Green. I had cycled around 450 miles during our first year together!

"When they signed up to do a national tour of *Snow White*, with Ruby in the title role and Bernie as Prince Rupert, the show was spread out over nearly two years, and the initial advance work proved for me a marathon of over 1,000 miles in 11 days. It was a pleasure to be doing the journeying on behalf of two people to whom I had become so attached."

Eric fully understood the need to bring in some cash quickly. Keith Devon had secured a booking for Ruby in Margate for the summer season with Hughie Green, whose show, *Hughie Green's Spectacular*, was being staged at the Winter Garden. There was also a cabaret date in a club in Manchester, which Ruby did with Bernie (a first for her) and the prospect of a tour with *Snow White and the Seven Dwarfs*, produced by Fred Woodward. Eric arranged for some publicity photos to be taken by Mark Gudgeon which, Ruby says, "did me proud, introducing just a hint of sophistication". These were used for her new record, *Pianissimo*, which, however, didn't do as well as they had hoped but which, with another new Irish LP with Norrie Paramor called *Irish and Proud Of It*, nevertheless kept the royalties coming in.

Eric also arranged for some family photographs to be taken on Julie's second birthday. These were widely used, with captions ranging from "Singing girl-next-door is star and housewife now" to "Ruby Murray, wife and mother, makes her comeback".

The Press loved the "comeback" line but Ruby laughs as she says: "I hadn't actually stopped singing, and I was making a reasonable living, although obviously nothing like it had been just a few years before. I never knew where I'd come back from, but at that time I did need the publicity."

She and Bernie, and Julie and her nanny Jane, rented a flat in Birchington, near Margate, for the summer and Ruby began rehearsals for the Hughie Green spectacular. As part of their act, Ruby sang *Mr. Wonderful* in front of a cocktail bar where a figure was seated with his back to the audience. As she finished, he turned around — to be revealed as Bernie. He came forward, sang and danced with her and brought many sentimental smiles to the faces of the audiences who had seen the happy family pictures in the local Press.

At the end of the season, and before setting out on tour with *Snow White*, Ruby and Bernie became partners with Tom "Rusty" Hood in a health and gymnasium club in Queensway,

London. This, as well as hoping to help with their financial situation, was part of the new "energetic" image that had been agreed between Ruby, Bernie and the management and publicity factors. At a Press reception for the official launching of the partnership they were all photographed lifting weights — Tom, Eric, Bernie and Ruby. "I had the lightest weight available", she said.

It was a pity that most of the papers which reported the event prefaced it with: "Ruby Murray, who has not had a record in the charts for two years ... " Says Ruby: "It was hurtful but something I was beginning to get used to. Of all the girl singers who were battling with me in the Top Twenty in the Fifties, only Petula Clark and Shirley Bassey went on to become international stars. Most of the rest of us carried on earning a reasonable living for a while after our kind of music was no longer the best-seller it had been."

For Eric it was the longest and most enjoyable trip he had ever undertaken for the Burgesses — London to Portsmouth, followed by Portsmouth to Stratford. Then it was on to Birmingham, Nantwich, Chester, Birkenhead and Liverpool. On again to Rochdale, Bradford, Harrogate, Gateshead, Newcastle-upon-Tyne. Working back down south, Eric arrived at Southsea in time for the opening of *Snow White* at the King's Theatre.

The King's, designed by Frank Matcham and opened in 1907 by Henry Irving, son of the famous actor, also named Henry Irving, was built on the site of a grocery shop on the corner of Albert Road. The main foyer occupies the space of the shop and the stage area is over a spring; to this day it sometimes has to be pumped clear of water. It is a large theatre and Ruby's voice is very small. She projects her voice far better now than she did in 1962 when *Snow White* opened there on 16th October

A radio microphone was installed in her bra and the rest of the company were told that if they wanted to benefit from the amplification they would need to stay as close to Ruby as the action allowed. This produced some strange grouping on the stage, especially when some of the cast were gazing intently at her bosom and very definitely talking to it!

Full-sized microphones had been in existence for a very long time, but the tiny concealed ones were still experiencing teething troubles. Controlled from offstage, Ruby had no come-back when just as she was enunciating "Prithee Father..." a deep gruff voice boomed out all over the theatre, "Taxi number 77, go to the corner of Chelsea Road and pick up Mrs. Smith."

The audience fell about, and so did most of the cast, until the next message, when the stage manager quickly switched off the erring microphone and Ruby's words became lost in the vastness of the theatre. Her lips moved but it seemed no words were coming out or, in the parlance of the piece, issuing forth. During the interval they examined the mike, and Ruby, thinking it was still switched off, said despairingly to the stage manager: "It's ridiculous, I can't go on like this..." Of course it was switched on and her words reached every corner of the auditorium...

It happened again at Bradford Alhambra during the tour, but on that occasion the tiny throat mike picked up some local police messages. While Ruby, looking suitably wistful, sweetly sang *Some Day My Prince Will Come*, a man's voice echoed throughout the theatre with "V for Victor Able calling Z for Zebra One. Please proceed to Tennyson Place..."

In the production, Grimm, the huntsman, who the Queen had told to kill Snow White, was played by Llewellyn Davies, a legitimate actor. Most of the rest of the cast were from the world of variety, revue and the recording studio. So when Llewellyn had a duel with Prince Rupert, played by Bernie, he was so realistic and enthusiastic about the part that Bernie used to stagger off, groaning: "One day he's going to really kill me."

Snow White toured for a year, with just a two-month break for a pre-booked pantomime at Chester, and Ruby has happy and amusing memories of it. There was the time when she was on stage as Snow White supposedly gazing out of a window, when an elderly lady, carrying a handbag and an umbrella, appeared between the scenic backdrop and the window. Ruby recognised her as an old friend, but was amazed to see her there. Possibly the audience were, too. Apparently the lady had called at the stage door and been told by the doorman, who also knew her: "Ruby's still on stage. Her dressing room's the other side of the stage. Go and make yourself comfortable until she comes off!"

Another scene has Snow White falling on to her bed. The dwarfs then pull the curtains around her but she has some time to wait while the action is still going on outside. Ruby had often taken several bites of the apple in an absent-minded way while waiting, but at one particular performance when the dwarfs drew back the curtains and said, "Look, Snow White has taken a bite of the poisoned apple", she was holding the core, and there was no trace of apple left. They all fell about laughing, the seven dwarfs holding their sides and the audience delighted, too. Ruby loves doing pantomime; her favourite is *Cinderella*, "because Cinders is the best girl's part in pantomime and it's a lovely fairy story anyway".

When she did *Cinderella* at The Pavilion, Torquay, in 1960 the diamante slippers were being sent down from London in time for the dress rehearsal; until then they had used ordinary shoes. The special slippers duly arrived and the dress rehearsal began. The Press and a few other selected people were there when the moment came for Prince Charming and Dandini to arrive at Baron Hardup's house with the glass slipper on a velvet cushion to fit the foot of Cinderella, played by Ruby. On went the slipper — or rather it didn't because it wouldn't!

"It fits, it fits!" cried the prince, while Ruby frantically tried to push her foot into the glittering glass slipper which was far too small. There followed an urgent telephone call to London for a replacement to be sent down for the following day. That year *Cinderella* set a box office record for the Pavilion that has never been broken.

The *Snow White* tour of 1962-63 stopped at Christmas for Ruby and Bernie to play Princess Valentine and Jack, the Miller's Son, in *Puss in Boots*. Impressionist Peter Goodwright and Alex Munro were also in the cast. Julie and her nanny travelled with them and they all dressed warmly when they went out to help the toddler make snowmen during an exceptionally cold winter.

Just before Christmas, Ruby had appeared on TV again in a Dickie Henderson series called *The Leprechaun*. After it she was asked for her comments on pop singer Helen Shapiro's rise to fame, why Helen hadn't had a record in the charts for months, and how Ruby felt about her own career. "Success is a wonderful thing", Ruby said. "I'm very happy about everything that happened, but my life is a lot easier now than when I was at the top."

The media hadn't finished with her yet, however. She recorded a song called *I'll Walk the Rest of the Way* about a woman who had a lover and alighted from his car at the corner of her road so her husband wouldn't see her. Jean Metcalfe said on *Juke Box Jury*: "We can't have dear Ruby, who has this sweet dairymaid image, spoiling it by singing songs like this." On the flip side was a song with lyrics by Ruby — she has written several songs — and music by Colin Keys, called *I'm In Love With The Boy Next Door.*

When *Puss In Boots* finished, Ruby and Bernie returned to touring with *Snow White*, taking it from Aberdeen to Dublin and beyond. Everywhere it had a steady box office. The run finished at the end of August 1963 and the couple moved into their new home in Wootton which had since been renovated.

CHAPTER 11

Mourning Alma

The show must go on. Ruby and Bernie did another tour to Aden, where Ruby again met brother Jack, now happily back in the RAF. Then it was on to the Persian Gulf and Kenya. They left Julie at home with her nanny. On their return Jean and Peter Barbour, the stilt-walkers who they had met in *Snow White,* came to stay while they looked around for a house in the same area. They eventually found one opposite the Burgesses, and this was to prove a boon to Ruby a little later.

Meanwhile Ruby and Bernie tried hard to make their marriage work as well as the publicity reports in the papers said it did, and within a few months Ruby found she was pregnant again. She was quite ill in the early stages and Dr. Watson was concerned about her working — she was booked for a summer season in Great Yarmouth. But she convinced him that it would "take her out of herself", and he agreed it would do no harm as long as she took things as easy as she could.

This time Bernie didn't come; he had started in management. Ruby rented a house for her, Julie and the nanny a few miles outside Great Yarmouth. Bernie visited at weekends, but was kept busy organising Ruby Murray Enterprises and the clients he had taken on during the week. Ruby felt very neglected. With Bernie and the car still in Wootton she travelled to the theatre on a bus each day, which caused more resentment.

It was a good summer season. When it finished, Ruby returned to Wootton to wait for the arrival of her second child. Dr. Watson again advised her of complications, so it was to be another caesarean — "My poor tummy now looks like a map of Ireland!" she says. Timothy John was born on 3rd February

1965, even more jaundiced than Julie had been, but again so beautiful. There was an additional worry because they thought for a time they would have to change all his blood. "It's nothing to worry about", the medical staff told Ruby — who promptly doubled the amount of time she spent worrying. When they told her Timothy John also had an open valve in his heart she was "going mad with apprehension". However the doctors decided to wait as the fault sometimes rights itself within the first year — as it proved in Tim's case. They also changed their minds about the blood transfusion for him, but Ruby had to take him to the hospital every six weeks for a check-up. Of one thing there was no doubt — his lungs were in tip-top order, "Julie had hardly cried at all, yet Tim cried all the time, mostly at the top of his voice!" says Ruby.

The need to earn some money was still great and Ruby took on several south coast engagements while Tim was tiny — taking him, Julie and nanny along, too. Then she had the chance to tour the northern clubs. So, leaving the children at home with Bernie, who was running his management business from the cottage, she set off with her pianist, Colin Keys, for Sunderland, where her first date was at Wetherall's Club.

She remembers the Sunderland trip as a wretched experience. "It was terribly difficult trying to adjust to clubs after working in theatres. Most of the customers were tough businessmen who wanted somebody far more glamorous and sexy than I was. They made it obvious that *Galway Bay* and *A Little Bit Of Heaven* were their idea of hell. I needed Bernie desperately because I didn't know how to handle the situation, but he was busy back in Northampton, and the nanny was looking after the children. Much as I love showbusiness this wasn't what I wanted to be doing."

The summer found Ruby in Bridlington for the season. Again she had the nanny and the children with her in a rented bungalow, and Bernie came for the opening show and most weekends. On the bill were Joe "Mr. Piano" Henderson and singer Vince Hill. It was a happy show but not a successful one at the box office. Tim was christened during that summer at one of the oldest churches in the country — at Burton Agnes, near Bridlington. From the photographs of the occasion that appeared in the newspapers you wouldn't have thought there was a happier family in the land; but beneath the united facade were deep sadness and resentment.

Bernie would telephone every night at 10.45pm to ask how the show went and how the children were. Ruby would be there to answer his call. Then the late Archie Purdie, who was also in the show, would take her to visit Vince Hill and his wife Pat, or go to Joe Henderson's place, where they gathered to eat, drink, and talk.

"Sometimes they'd all come back to my place and we'd play records. It was all quite innocent", said Ruby, "but Bernie wouldn't have approved. It was a lot of fun, except that I was steadily getting used to taking more drinks than I had before, wines, sherries and brandies, and I sometimes had more than I could handle."

Back in Wootton, Bernie broached the subject of Ruby giving up showbusiness. It made her realise how much she loved life in the theatre and among theatre folk and she refused to give it all up. Apart from the money, she couldn't visualise herself settling down without this element in her life. "It was also my salvation when I was unhappy. I knew I was drinking too much but that would have happened at home, too, maybe even more than it did away because there would have been more time for it. I *never* drank until *after* the performance."

Life in The White House at Oxshott, Surrey, had been "amongst real, kindly people. I never met a snob amongst them and they had everything. They loved me as a neighbour and I loved them. When I went on tour, my neighbours, Tony and Isabel, used to come over and say, 'We'll send your mail on to you'.

"They were all so kind, yet when I moved to that little village near Northampton I met more would-be snobs, and they gave me a lot of pain. They hated to see me being able to lie-in because I often worked until 3am or 4am when I was working the clubs and doing cabaret. Some were jealous that I could afford a housekeeper and a nanny for the children, but it didn't mean a thing to me. I was doing a job, my job, and I needed staff like that to keep the house running properly. But they made life impossible sometimes, and that was apart from the unhappiness which was threatening our marriage. Bernie couldn't understand why I couldn't make it with the neighbours. Not being a woman, he didn't understand all the little snide things they were doing to me. And, of course, he was from the area and I was a stranger there."

Peter and Jean Barbour were now living almost opposite the Burgesses, and Ruby began to spend more and more time with them. Record sales were hardly as healthy as they had been, but they were steady. And each summer there was a season somewhere, which allowed Ruby to have the children with her while she was working. She was at the Tower Ballroom, Great Yarmouth, when she became friends with Iris Chapple and Jean McGrath, a dancer and a swimmer who were in the show. Both practised the philosophy of Sat Suma, and each appeared to be healthy and well-balanced. If you live by Sat Suma you must not eat animal flesh or anything connected with it and Ruby listened to their theories when she was eating a steak one day and they asked her incredulously: "Do you realise what you are doing?"

When Ruby asked them about this different way of life they told her of all the impurities she was taking into her body. Impressed by Iris and Jean's health and vitality, she read books about it and decided to give it a go. "I was living on mushrooms and tomatoes on toast", she said, "and from never having been fat I got thinner and thinner. Bernie became very worried. To make up for the lack of vitamins in the diet you have to take B12 tablets and drink cups of black molasses, which I couldn't face without being violently ill. Even the smell of it revolts me, so I missed out on that. Alcohol was not allowed, and I thought this would be good discipline for me because I knew I was drinking too much. As it turned out I did not stick rigidly to that rule."

Back home after the Yarmouth season, Ruby soon reverted to eating all kinds of food again, much to her husband's relief. Keith Devon was still Ruby's agent, but Bernie, in his management role, also got her some bookings which, Ruby says, "obviously didn't make for a harmony threesome". Said Keith: "If she had been handled properly she would have been one of the greatest stars in the country. Maybe it would have been better if domestic duties hadn't cropped up. She turned down several important engagements just after her marriage because of this. But she was young and in love, and you can't fight that."

Ruby remained one of Keith's three favourite performers until he died — the others being Joan Regan and boogie pianist Winifred Attwell. In October 1966 Ruby had a chance to go to America again on a tour for Bill Fullem; Marie went with her as secretary/companion on a visit that included New York, San Francisco, Chicago and Boston and several smaller places.

When they reached Chicago, Ruby recalled her previous appearance at the Keyman's Club in front of a hostile audience. This time trouble began before they even left the airport when the automatic doors jammed. "That's an omen", said Ruby, who is extremely superstitious. She will never wear green on stage and when working in the theatre insists: "No green lights and no revolving glitter balls", the latter because they make her feel dizzy. If she wears a new dress or shoes and doesn't go down well on stage she will never wear them again.

However the stuck doors were soon sorted out and Ruby and Marie were driven to a motel several miles out of Chicago. Ruby was working at the Keyman's Club as before, but now it had a new name and new management. The motel was several miles out of Chicago and quite terrifying in its loneliness.

"It was the time of the Boston Strangler", said Ruby, "and with the wind howling around the place we were both scared."

Ruby piled all their cases up against the door, then Marie phoned Bill, who had made the booking, and told him this simply wouldn't do and they wanted to come into Chicago.

Ruby asked Bill, who was also Irish, what sort of songs they were expecting and what to wear. He said: "Sure an' it's a folk night tonight, Ruby. Just wear a wee jumper and skirt and you'll be fine."

She put away the glittery stage dress, put on a jumper and skirt and they went down to the club. But there was a group on when they arrived and, to Ruby's astonishment, the girl singer with them was wearing a long dress, covered from head to toe in green sequins. "All shimmering she was, and there was I, supposed to be the star of the show and dressed in a jumper and skirt!"

However it turned out to be a good night, with a warm audience adding encouragement. The Chicago concert was bang in the middle of the tour and Ruby and Marie did quite a bit of sightseeing. In San Francisco they explored the Chinese Quarter and Fisherman's Wharf, scoffing pounds of sausages and devouring pancakes with syrup for breakfast!

"It was great fun", said Ruby. "Of course I missed the children, but if I hadn't been in America I would have been working in England and I knew they were being taken proper care of." She also hoped that when she returned things might be better between her and Bernie: "They do say 'Absence makes the heart grow fonder', though in my case that didn't happen." Although Ruby was drinking fairly heavily (when she wasn't working) she had yet to touch whisky. But on that tour she was initiated. It was in New York, and she was with an Irish band run by Harry (Mitch) Mitchell. "I knew him from way back, we kind of grew up together. He's a great singer and pianist." They did the show, and afterwards all of them went to a club where someone showed Ruby a newspaper from England with a picture of Alma Cogan and a report of her death at the early age of 34.

Ruby and Alma didn't like each other. They moved in the

same circles but, although they never said so in public, they didn't get on. "She used to take the mickey out of me", said Ruby. "Alma was very sophisticated. We used to see each other at various parties and people always asked us to sing a duet, which we did. But she made fun of me, sometimes quite cruelly. She thought I didn't realise it, but of course I did, though I wasn't prepared to make a scene. I can get on with most people, but we were so different and it was a mutual dislike.

"But when she died, it hurt. I cried my eyes out because she was young and a great artiste. I forgot all about us not liking each other and I cried and cried, and poor Harry got so upset. He said 'You'd better have a whisky to calm you down.' After about three of them I was legless and still crying. So he and Marie led me across the street to where we were staying and they put me to bed, still crying. I passed out, crying, and apparently Harry said to Marie, 'I thought you told me she didn't like Alma Cogan, didn't get on with her.' And Marie said, 'She didn't.' 'Well', he said, 'I'd hate to see her if someone she liked died!'"

Ruby returned to Britain to find the same situation in her marriage as before. Bernie was trying several businesses at this time. Bookmaking didn't work out, so he went into partnership with former footballer Theo Foley in a little fried chicken-and-chips takeaway. But, whether he liked it or not, Bernie was involved in showbusiness — and when he was asked to build up the run-down Cresta Club in Birmingham, he took it on and made it work. He also sorted out the entertainment, booking singers Eartha Kitt and Dorothy Squires among many illustrious names, and the Cresta became one of the biggest and best clubs in the Midlands.

Ruby says now: "When Bernie did that he was standing in his own right, because it is very hard for a man to stand behind a woman and take it. It needs a special kind of man and there's not too many of them about. I understood Bernie's feelings then, as I do today."

CHAPTER 12

Black humour, white lie

Ruby was again in Yarmouth in 1967 for the summer show. This was her fourth year there and she felt at home. Bernie stayed in Northampton with his business; Ruby took Julie and Tim and their new nanny, Maureen Wells, with her. They stayed in a house quite close to the town, with many chalets in the grounds. Almost the entire company were there, which made for parties and entertaining virtually every night.

The show also starred comedian Joe Baker, Freddie Garrity of Freddie and the Dreamers, The Tornadoes, Toni Dalli and Devi Shawn. Ruby's old friend Val Doonican was at one of the other theatres and during the season they did a broadcast together. Ruby also went to dinner with him and his wife, Lynette, with whom she had shared digs when they were in pantomime together nearly a decade before.

Drink was plentiful at the evening get-togethers, and when Bernie arrived unexpectedly one evening he chose not to go to the party afterwards. Ruby hadn't been sleeping well and the doctor had given her some sleeping pills, to be taken just before going to bed and not before going to a party. Bernie insisted on Ruby staying home but she had other ideas. She popped a sleeping pill into his tea, and he was asleep very quickly. She then climbed out of the window and went to the party.

"I needed the laughs and the music and the frivolity of it all. It was all pretty harmless. We had something to eat and drink, talked shop and gossiped. It wasn't an orgy by any means." She returned to the house, using the same method as for her departure — the window. Bernie was still fast asleep, so she returned to bed without him knowing at the time that she had even been out.

"It kept me sane and a reasonable human being at a time when our marriage was getting worse. I knew parties and drinking weren't the answer, but most of the time Bernie wasn't there and I got into the habit of it. I never left the children alone. Maureen, our nanny, was marvellous. She always knew where I was."

When the season finished Ruby did a Canadian tour and Marie accompanied her. Chart-topping singer David Whitfield shared top billing and they had a successful tour, sprinkled with a fair share of parties. The one she remembers best should have taken place in America. They were to cross Niagara Falls to go to it, but when they found they needed a work permit to enter the USA, the party was brought to them instead!

Ruby's records were still selling although, unlike David Whitfield's, she had none in the charts. Then *Sooner Or Later* was featured on the TV game show *The Golden Shot* on St. Patrick's Day, and her record sales took a turn for the better.

1969 saw her once again in Canada, this time for an Irish television show, *The Pig and Whistle*. It became a family affair when Bernie and the children came, too, and they both tried hard to patch up their ailing marriage. All the publicity pictures showed a happy family enjoying themselves, and for the duration of the Canadian trip it almost became true. Later they went on holiday to Spain with Don Crockett, a comedian Bernie was promoting, and his wife Moira; but Bernie and Ruby were two separate people instead of two separate halves of a whole. They both knew the relationship wasn't working.

Christmas 1968 was spent away from home. A booking for cabaret in a hotel in Lagos, Nigeria, seemed too good to miss; they still needed the money and secretly Ruby was dreading the rows she knew would happen if they were all home together. The only problem was that Nigeria was being ravaged by civil war at the time. Ruby's pianist was Bob Francis, who she had not met before. Bernie drove her to the airport and exhorted Bob to look after her and make sure she didn't drink too much! Her agent had given her a bag filled with Christmas decorations because he said they couldn't get them at the hotel because of the fighting going on. The flight took 20 hours, and they swapped stories and laughs (and had a few drinks) before landing in Lagos. The temperature was over 100 in the shade but, because it was so cold when she left England, Ruby was still wearing fur boots and a fur jacket.

She was longing to change into something cooler, but the airport official in charge wouldn't let them through because, he said, they had filled out a form wrongly. He also wouldn't allow them to alter it. He simply said: "You go back right away! Next plane." They refused, they argued and they pleaded, but he was adamant: "Back on next plane." They were there an hour, in the sweltering heat, Ruby still wearing her boots and fur jacket, afraid to take them off in case the official got the wrong idea!

With the sweat literally pouring from her, she asked if she could telephone the Federal Palace Hotel where they were booked in. Finally the official agreed. "Come", he said, and led them through to a telephone which was housed in a little shed. Ruby telephoned the hotel manager to find out why nobody had been there to meet them and sort it out. "If someone doesn't come soon they're going to send us back", she warned.

There were apologies from the management, and the promise that someone would come immediately. "Just stand your ground and refuse to go, and we will get there as quickly as possible", Ruby was told.

Walking back to the main building, the official — tall, black and imposing — asked: "You make it all right? I stamp?" Bob looked at Ruby, and Ruby looked at him, and Bob said: "I think, yes, I'm sure, he's offering us a bribe. Or rather, asking for one. What do you think we should do?" It was like a cartoon sequence. They were almost back in the main building and she was frantically trying to work out how much he wanted, when Bob whispered, "How much do you think, £300?"

"Yes, three or four hundred should do it", Ruby whispered.

Bob coughed and turned to the official. "How much do you want?" he asked.

The official replied: "£1."

Ruby and Bob looked disbelievingly at each other and repeated together: "£1?"

"Yes, £1", said the official.

"I nearly fainted on the spot", Ruby says now. "I think he'd have sold us the whole of Africa for a fiver."

The next stop was the customs shed. Ruby, who was drinking brandy at that time, and Bob, who was on gin, had brought extra bottles with them. The bags were opened, the gin and brandy noted, and the bags closed, marked and passed. Ruby picked up the carrier bag of Christmas decorations for the hotel and they walked on. They had only gone a few yards when someone tapped Ruby on the shoulder. He was a man of few words. "Come", he said. Back they trooped to the customs shed where he wanted to know what was in the carrier bag. Relieved and almost light-hearted now, Ruby said: "Christmas decorations for the Federal Palace Hotel." But the man was not convinced.

"Show me", he insisted.

She hadn't looked in the bag. She had simply taken it from her agent and not opened it once. She did so now and the first things to come out were dozens of balloons. They all had little black sambos printed on them. The official poked them with his stick, then pulled out another bag.

"What those?" he asked. Ruby opened the bag and said: "Streamers."

He repeated her words: "Streamers. Streamers. No understand your English. Explain."

She said: "Well, you have dinner. You sit at a long table, and after you've had your dinner, and coffee and drink, you — you throw them over each other."

Looking back over almost 30 years Ruby recalls: "I was beginning to cry with laughter at the word picture I was painting. I mean, taking part in an activity like that when you're at a party is one thing, but trying to tell someone from another culture and make it sound logical was almost beyond me. But worse was to come, because he then said solemnly, 'Still don't understand. Show me'."

So they opened the bag and Ruby, Bob, and the solemn-looking official — "the chief guy", as Bob called him, — stood there throwing streamers over each other. This went on for several minutes, which Ruby said felt like hours, and she and Bob were sweltering now in the heat and their thick clothes, when suddenly the official's face broke into a big smile and he said: "I like. I confiscate." And he took all the decorations.

The show was a great success and when Ruby returned to England it was to an offer for a musical to be produced at the Connaught theatre, Worthing, and to be called *Blues Avenue*. Says Ruby: "I was asked 'Would you mind playing a mother?' What a question! I *was* a mother, I was 32 now, no longer a naive nineteen-year-old with her first record in the Top Twenty. In fact I hadn't had a record in the charts for almost two years; yet I hesitated", she said.

What bothered her most was whether she could cope as an actress. The money would have been small in comparison to her record and variety earnings, but Ruby says she would have been happy to risk it if she truly thought she could make a go of it.

"I remember the comedienne Beryl Reid telling me that when she was first offered the play that was to change her career, *The Killing of Sister George*, it was for a very small amount in comparison with what she was earning in variety and summer seasons. Her agent tried to talk her out of it but she insisted she wanted to give it a try; she has never regretted her decision."

But Ruby still wasn't sure. "Beryl is a superb actress", she said, "and she had done a considerable amount of character work already, whereas I — well, I was a singer, I had always been a singer, and I was perfectly happy to continue if the public wanted me." She told her publicity agent, Eric Braun: "If I fell flat on my face, as I might well do, it will only damage an already ailing career."

The publicity at that time was concerned with the togetherness of the family, and concentrated on the happiness they all enjoyed. Ruby found it indescribably sad, but knew there was nothing she could do to spoil the image. The other publicity myth was that the offers were coming thick and fast and she didn't know which to take. Which was also not really true.

"Both Bernie and I were trying so hard to make our marriage work, and it was a harmless enough white lie", she said. But Keith Devon, who was still her agent, turned down the musical offer, and instead accepted one with President Records.

About this time the local Irish Society invited her to Rhodesia (now Zimbabwe). Ruby went, with Marie as accompanist, and discovered what a marvellous land Rhodesia was — though when they first arrived they wondered!

They had the address where they were to stay but when they climbed into the taxi and asked for their destination, the driver looked at them and warned: "You don't want to go there."

"Yes", they chorused, and showed him their booking slips. He argued with them for a while, but they were adamant; so he shrugged and took them, albeit reluctantly. The place where they were booked to stay turned out to be a brothel. "There were black and white boys and girls running up and down all night", Ruby said. "Marie and I decided to sleep in the same room, although we had been allotted one each, and the following morning she rang up and had us transferred to a proper hotel!"

Ruby, who is such an extrovert, enjoyed the hospitality and friendliness of the Rhodesians. She and Marie went to several barbecues and house parties — and it was at one of these that they were invited to dinner with Ian Smith (then Premier of Rhodesia), his wife Janet and two other guests. Ruby laughs now about the muddle she got into with her chicken. "Mr.

Smith was so kind", she says. "He saw I was in trouble and he came over and said, 'Let me help you, my dear', and he cut it up for me."

Ruby has a low opinion of her intellect — unfairly because she has a quick grasp of situations and facts. She remains full of admiration for Ian Smith. "I'm not a political creature", she said, "but having seen him visiting hospitals, schools and an open prison, and getting on with lots of people, I thought him an honest and dedicated man.

"He doesn't smile a lot in public because of the plastic surgery which makes up half his face; he was shot down during the war when he was a fighter pilot in the RAF. But he has tremendous charm and consideration and my memories of that evening will always stay with me."

Another memory of Rhodesia is a humorous one and concerns a peeping tom. When they moved from the brothel to the hotel the night after they arrived, they were put into a little *rhondaval* (round house). These were dotted about the grounds and were extremely comfortable. Undressing one night, Marie saw these two huge eyes watching through the window, and she screamed.

It happened again the following night and the police came with their fingerprint box. They set it up, put powder on the window sill, then went with Ruby and Marie to Ruby's early evening show — she was doing two shows, at 6pm and midnight. They all had a few drinks after the show, returned to the hotel — and found that the fingerprint box had been stolen! However, the girls weren't bothered by the peeping tom again during their stay.

Ruby remembers the moving experience of visiting a black "wake". "I'll never forget either the picture or the sounds of the night, with mourners singing outside the *rhondaval.* It was hauntingly beautiful."

The cake for Ruby's 21st birthday was decorated with the main theme from her biggest hit, "Softly, Softly".

"Fez the music", — with Tommy Cooper at Blackpool, 1957.

Ruby, as most fans remember her... singing her heart out in the spotlight on a TV show.

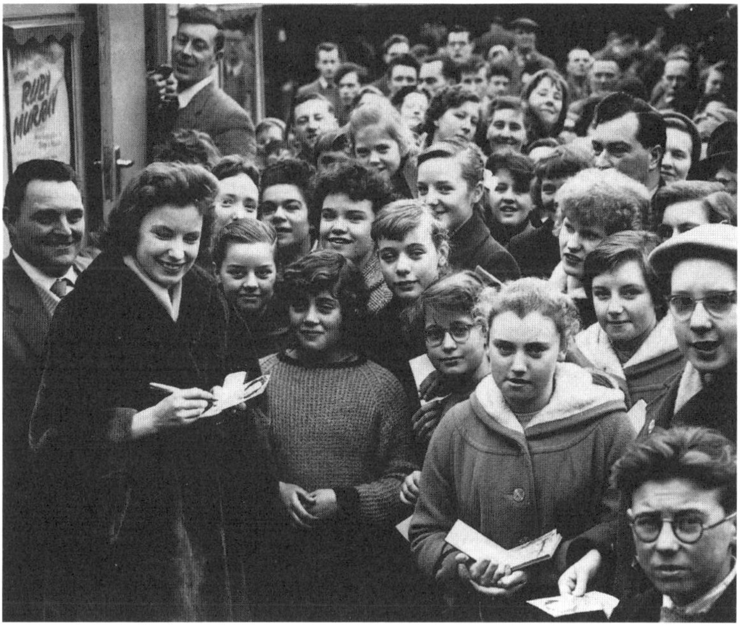

A sea of faces, a throng of admirers... Ruby signs autographs before a show.

Hats off from the Navy. Ruby made goodwill tours of Rosyth and military bases at home and abroad during the Fifties.

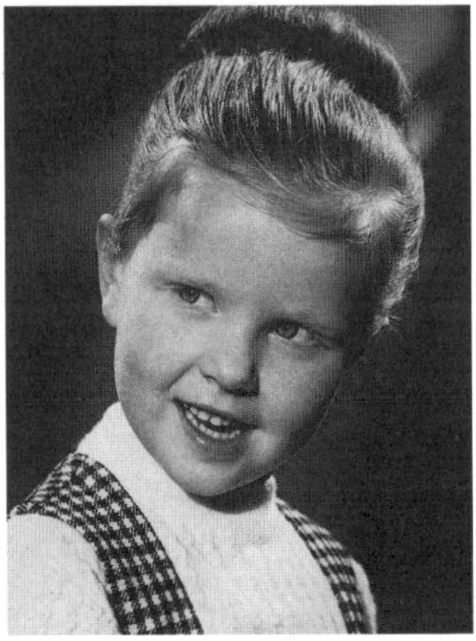

Opposite page: *(top), a delightful picture of Ruby with Tim in the baby frame.*

Below, a serious Tim, aged three (left), and a studio portrait of Julie.

Right, the three of us ... Ruby, Julie and Bernie.

Below, family gathering ... Winifred holds Julie, surrounded by the proud mother and father, and Ruby's sister Patsy.

A night on the town with second husband Ray Lamar.

Opposite: *Ruby as Madonna. It was claimed that the American singer had more hits in the charts than Ruby in her prime. The Irish girl did a brilliant take-off on TV.*

Above, with two old show business friends. Larry Grayson points the finger at Dora Bryan.

Ruby as she is today, looking back on a life filled with happiness... and heartbreak.

CHAPTER 13

"That's not Big Dan..".

Back from Rhodesia, she and Bernie made a concentrated effort to make their marriage work. Before the trip Ruby had appeared on Bernard Braden's TV show *Braden's Week* along with Guy Mitchell, Donald Peers, Lita Roza, David Whitfield, Reg Dixon and Eve Boswell. She sang *Softly, Softly,* and President Records offered her a contract. As she hadn't made a new record for nearly two years she welcomed the chance and Mike and Joy Segal wrote a new song, called *Change Your Mind*, for her.

President promotions man Cyril Black kept her busy making personal appearances, signing records, and giving interviews, and when they learned that *Change Your Mind* had entered the Radio Luxembourg charts at No. 23 they held a champagne reception, attended by the cream of the recording world. However, it didn't make the Top Twenty, although it seemed to be a favourite choice on most of the record programmes. Ruby made an LP for President, using *Change Your Mind* as the title song. Michael Thornton, who had recently resigned as film and drama critic of the *Sunday Express* to concentrate on books, was asked to write the sleeve notes.

He says: "A date was made for me to meet Ruby at a pub in the Bayswater Road. Eric Braun came along, and brought with him the Irish character actress Bee Duffel. Ruby arrived, bang on the dot, looking extremely young and mod (she was then 35) in knee-high, white boots and a mini-length purple coat with a fur hood. In this swinging Seventies outfit, she bore little resemblance to the rather gauche girl I first remembered from the Fifties, and I was interested to note that although people in the pub glanced at her curiously, sensing she was 'someone', there was little or no recognition of who she was.

"I rather fancied myself as a photographer in those days and had brought along my Rolleiflex, so we crossed over into Hyde Park, where I took two reels of film. One, with close-ups of Ruby with the purple fur hood framing her face, against a background of green leaves, was used as the sleeve photograph on her new album. Maddeningly, President Records either lost, or at least never sent me back the colour transparencies taken of her alone that day, which is sad because we all thought them among the best we'd seen of her.

"Ruby wrote to thank me for the sleeve notes and to say that she loved the colour photograph I had taken. President Records seemed to me a rather curious organisation and I remember that when I eventually got paid, the cheque was drawn on the Bank of Nova Scotia, which struck me as a little bizarre, but wholly in character."

Soon after, Ruby received a phone call to ask if she was interested in meeting a couple of men who were keen to promote her career. Ruby agreed. After all, what harm could it do. It might even do a lot of good. She always insisted that she had never asked for, or even wanted, the kind of fame she had in the beginning, but her career was in need of a boost and it seemed fate had lent a hand. She met the men at London's Hilton Hotel one morning. One of her songwriters was also there, and they talked with the two men about a show to be put on at the London Palladium, then went on to records and the charts. At which point they asked her pointedly if they could "buy" her record in to the charts. This was a practice often used by singers who couldn't make it on their own merits.

Ruby's answer was typical. She told them she had never done that sort of thing before and wasn't going to start now. Others at the meeting then suggested the song being "bought". One said it could be arranged easily for around £150 a week, but Ruby maintained she wasn't interested in any kind of deal and didn't want to know, and on that note they adjourned for lunch. It was pouring with rain and they had a problem finding a taxi for her, but they managed it eventually and Ruby went home and thought that was the end of the matter.

Two weeks later she discovered that the two "charming gentlemen" who had taken them out to lunch that day were reporters for the *News of The World*, investigating and exposing bribes involving radio and television plugging.

Ruby knew she hadn't committed herself to anything dishonest, but was still worried because she realised how easy it was for the public to grasp the wrong idea when they saw something in a newspaper. Any remark could be deliberately taken out of context in the "interests" of journalism. Ruby mostly had good dealings with reporters and newspapers, but when she saw the *News of The World* headline on its "Payola revelations" series she felt like suing the newspaper.

"Curious Case Of Ruby Murray's Comeback", it stated in large, thick, black type. It was quite a long article, but at least it correctly stated that Ruby had had nothing to do with any bribe to get her latest record into the charts.

In fact Ruby never received a penny for making that record, nor for any copies which were legitimately sold! The article was accompanied by a photograph showing Ruby, Tony Saxon (song plugger), and Mike Segal (composer) waiting, glumly in the pouring rain, for a taxi. "It was not the best kind of publicity to have", said Ruby, "although later I had worse. But that was of my own making and this was not."

The next item on Ruby's agenda was a tour with David Whitfield, which took them to night clubs all over the country. Ruby was drinking far more now; she knew she needed to cut back, but drink gave her the courage to go on, no matter how unhappy she felt.

"Taking a drink used to make me sleep, and to say 'Oh, to hell with it! I'll get over it, it'll all come right.' But drink, of course, wasn't the answer, because when you wake up the problems are still there. And you've got a hangover, too, so you've another problem to add to them."

The tour was very successful. "Some hidden force saw me

through those times", she says now, "because they were very bad. My work helped tremendously. Being on stage, you had to put it all behind you and get on with what you were doing. And it was a marvellous tonic to find people still wanted me, that they still loved me." Ruby was constantly seeking reassurance. Lee Stevens took over from Keith Devon as Ruby's agent. He had always been a fan and as he grew to know her as a person and client he determined to find the right songs for her voice — itself the subject of endless discussion.

Her mother said the famous huskiness followed an operation on swollen glands when Ruby was just six weeks old. Ruby said: "Mum makes it all lovely and dramatic, with her trudging up the hill to the hospital in the snow with me, the baby in swaddling clothes, and slipping and clutching me to her bosom ..."

Ruby was born on 29th March, and six weeks from there takes us to the middle of May. Thick snow, though not impossible, is unlikely. But Ruby did have a gland operation at that tender age, and has a scar to prove it. It could have contributed, or even caused, that attractive and perfectly natural huskiness. She says she has had so many doctors looking down her throat and asking if she's in pain — and always the answer is no: It's the same when they ask if she suffers with many sore throats — in fact, she seldom catches a cold. Then the doctors ask if she will please leave her voice box to science!

Over the years Father John Caden had become a friend to Bernie as well as Ruby, and often left his car in their garage when he had to fly from Luton Airport on church business. On 23rd August, the date of Ruby and Bernie's wedding anniversary, he was there — and so was her sister Patsy — when Vinnie, a friend of her father's, telephoned to say Dan had been taken ill and was in hospital. Vinnie said he had gone into the operating theatre at mid-day; it was then 4pm. Ruby asked them to ring as soon as he recovered consciousness. She then replaced the receiver and looked at all the people gathered in her sitting room. "As I looked at Father John I *knew*", she said. "I thought, Dad's not going to come out of this; it's been too long. Vinnie had said something about a burst blood vessel. Patsy said, 'Four hours he's been down there…'"

The next phone call was to say he was dead. Ruby, who is a very emotional person, couldn't cry but Patsy couldn't stop crying. "Father John being there was a great comfort", Ruby said. "I had to let my mother know, and my brother Jack and my other sister Lilian, who was in Canada. And I kept calm through it all. I *still* couldn't cry, which might have helped, but it went deeper than that. And it was strange that it was my wedding anniversary and that he and Bernie had never got on." Ruby and Patsy flew over to Ireland the next day. "We had to go and see him every day in the funeral parlour. I didn't really want to go, but it's tradition. He was always so proud of himself, clean and tall, and very careful when he went out to always look smart. He combed his hair in a certain way because he was going bald on the top of his head, and that was all missing of course. My sister was screaming and crying and shouting 'That's not my daddy', and all the neighbours were around and one of them kept saying 'That's not Big Dan; oh, that's not Big Dan.' There's humour even in death. Although I was so upset, and I think I was a bit numb too, I found myself listening to them and thinking, 'I wonder, have we got the right body here?' Anyway, we all filed out and the next day we filed in again, and this same lady looked at him and said, 'Ah, he's looking much better today', and I thought, 'This could only be said in Ireland! How can he be looking much better today?' I said to her, 'Maybe at the weekend he'll be getting up and having a drink with us.'

"My dad would have laughed at that. He used to tell this story of a reputed newspaper report of a funeral: 'At the funeral of Mr. Shaun O'Shaughnessy his best friend Mr. Tim O'Leary lost his footing and fell into the open grave. He broke his leg and this cast an air of gloom over the occasion.' He had a wonderful sense of humour did my dad".

Big Dan's death was a tremendous blow to Ruby. She had

always been his favourite, and maybe the best bits of his nature were as near as she would ever come to her knight in shining armour. He fought for her career in the early days and had been so very proud when she made it to the top of her professional tree. She always had been his particular star and he loved it when she became the people's choice too.

"I don't think I ever got over his death", she said. "I think about him often and feel he's around...his spirit is still around. They say that in time you forget, but you really just get used to the idea that they're not there any more. I don't think you totally get over it."

When they returned from the funeral, there was a knock at the door and the man who supplied Dan with the mussels, which he loved, came in. "Where's Dan?" he asked. When they told him he almost passed out with shock. "He was so *healthy*", he said. Then someone stood up and said, "Come on, Dan's gone and we can't bring him back. Let the wake commence!" They all went to Dan's local, someone produced an accordion, the drink flowed, the baker next door brought in some soda bread and potato cakes and the stories and exploits of Big Dan brought laughter to mingle with the tears.

Bernie, who hadn't gone to the funeral, telephoned to know which plane to meet and was very put out when Ruby said she couldn't leave her family immediately, she was needed there. And Winnie, who hadn't gone to the funeral either, telephoned and they all tried to speak to her, but by that time the wine was taking its toll. Even Jack, who was usually very proper, was "tight" and Winnie said: "I can't understand you. None of you are making sense. Well, I'm telling you now that I'm having it put in my will that there will be no alcohol at my wake. Tea only, d'you hear me? You're not going to enjoy my departure!"

Now Ruby had no-one in her beloved Ireland except Marie. It seemed like the end of another chapter. She kept remembering the early days and it was too soon yet to recall them with anything but sadness that they had all gone.

CHAPTER 14

Ray of Sunshine

During the late Sixties and early Seventies Ruby toured the clubs during the winter and did a summer season from Easter until September.

Maureen Wells was now nanny to Julie and Tim. "Tim was two when I joined the household", she said. "It was my first job. Ruby was such fun and the children were adorable." Maureen stayed with them for three years and during that time she not only looked after the children but cooked, drove Ruby to gigs and "generally looked after things, which I love doing".

She was a schoolgirl when she first met Ruby in 1954. "I joined the fan club, wrote to her and went to see her perform whenever I could. I remember I knitted her a jumper for her birthday and there was a picture in the paper of her packing to go to Canada, and she was wearing my jumper. I felt so thrilled."

Ruby was glad to have someone with her at the clubs because she was paid in cash and felt safer with a companion alongside. Maureen recalls: "There were one or two whose cheques bounced, so we insisted on cash. Sometimes this meant waiting around for hours. Often we'd be there until 2am or 3am, then I'd drive Ruby home, where Bernie was looking after the children. I loved driving, too, and was only too happy to go with her, so it suited everyone."

Maureen remembers one evening at a club when she was standing at the back and the trio accompanying Ruby were way behind her in tempo. "Ruby was doing a circular wind-up movement with her arm to indicate to them to go faster, but instead they slowed up even more. I was nearly going frantic, because they were ruining her song, and I turned to the person standing next to me and said, 'This is awful, what a terrible pianist', and she replied icily: 'That is my husband.'"

She also recalls a dinner party she arranged when Ruby was at the Windmill in Great Yarmouth in 1967. "I knew Ruby liked everything romantic and soft, so, after the children were in bed, I set the table, which was by the window, polished the candlesticks until you could see your face in them, and placed three candles at strategic points on the table. When I heard them coming in I lit the candles and went to check on the meal. It was a hot night and they had left the front door open to let the air blow in. Someone opened the dining room door, and whoosh, suddenly the curtains were ablaze. Luckily, it was just the curtains that were damaged because we were all there and put it out very quickly, but it was frightening just the same."

Comedian Frank Carson recalls, with his own brand of Irish humour, a tour of the Highlands with Ruby during the Sixties. "We went by boat from the mainland of Scotland to Kirkwall in the Orkneys", he says, "and among the cast was Fu Chang, a Chinese magician born in Belfast. One day the boat hit a Force 8 gale and everybody on board was sick. Or dying, to be more exact. We were down below decks when an urgent message came from Fu Chang on the upper deck, asking to see Ruby. I said to Ruby, 'I'll go up with you, love.' She was being very ill. I wasn't too bad. I'd had two meals, one down and one up!

"We headed for the deck and it was a horrendous journey. Fu Chang was standing on the deck in his Chinese gear, and he said to me, 'Could you take a photo of Ruby and I, Frank?' My next words are unprintable!"

They made it to Kirkwall, steadied up on dry land, and did their show, "silently praying for fine, or at least calm, weather for the return journey", Ruby says. "But whichever it was, we knew that with Frank aboard we'd have plenty of laughs."

When she worked with Spike Milligan he used to phone her from his dressing room which was next door to hers. He always used different voices and pretended to be other people.

"It was quite outrageous, but such a lot of fun. I never dared say, 'I know it's you, Spike', in case it wasn't. The mimicking was so good."

In 1971 she was in Paignton, Devon, at the Festival Hall. Comedian Max Wall was also on the bill and they became good friends. "Apart from the fact that I think he was a great comic, we had at least two things in common. He had been in the showbiz wilderness for a time and also had matrimonial troubles."

Perhaps it was an exaggeration to say Ruby had been in the wilderness, but there were times when bookings were few and far between. "Max cheered me at a time when I badly needed it. We'd go and have a few drinks together after the show and have a few laughs."

It was during that season that Ruby again met Ray Lamar. Ray was now Delfont's entertainments manager for the West Country, and was based in Torquay. He and Ruby had met only once in the past 15 years, that was when she and Bernie went backstage at a production of *The Student Prince* which involved Ray. "Ray had loved me when I was young", she said, "and at the time I didn't realise how hurtful I had been. He knew my dad too, they had been friends, and I could talk to him about Dan's death."

In the intervening years Ray had married again, and had three beautiful children, two boys and a girl. But the marriage broke up and Ray and his wife were eventually divorced. He had also resigned from Delfonts and founded his own company, producing and presenting the revival of such musicals as *The Student Prince*, *The Desert Song* and *The Vagabond King*, with John Hanson in the lead. These proved very successful all around the country.

Said Ray: "Bernard Delfont took one of my musicals to the Palace Theatre in London, and it was agreed that I should return to the Delfont Organisation. In 1961 I went to Torquay to open the Princesss Theatre, and Mr. Delfont (now Lord Delfont) suggested I move permanently to the area and look after his two theatres there. I did this, and also ran the summer shows at the Babbacombe theatre with Max Bygraves' son, Anthony. It was an interesting life, and I was living in a part of the country which I have grown to love."

When Ruby appeared at Paignton she met Ray — and the years seemed to roll away. "We fell in love", he said simply, "all over again. After that we met as many times as we could."

Ruby recalls: "Ray was living apart from his second wife, Betty, and we saw a great deal of each other. We cried on each other's shoulders because we had both tried to make a go of our marriages. And because we knew each other so well as people, rather than as artistes, it wasn't a new beginning. We weren't trying to impress each other, and at first it was both a comforting and relaxing relationship. Gradually it became much, much more."

In between shows Ruby went home to Wootton, and Bernie and the children. Until they started school, the children had travelled with her; but after that they stayed at home with Bernie and a nanny. Maureen had left by then and there was a succession of others. "I was constantly in touch with them", Ruby said, "and I thought very deeply about giving up work and staying home all the time. But I have to be honest and say it wouldn't have worked. Bernie said 'Be a housewife, cook and clean.' But there's more to life for me than that, and it's singing. In any case, the children would have been at school all day and with Bernie out as well I'd have gone mad. Somehow, although I get so nervous before I go on, I have to sing."

Julie, who now manages a night club in London, says about her childhood: "My first memory is of sitting at a long table with the seven dwarfs — 'the dwarfies' I used to call them — and that would have been during the tour of *Snow White*. I always got on better with adults than with children. I couldn't relate to children and I was always with adults. I was a bit of a tomboy, too."

Maureen remembers Bernie always wanted Julie to look clean and feminine; but Julie wanted to rush about and climb trees in jeans and a teeshirt. "It was a constant battle. I always tried to have her wearing a dress when she went in to see her father."

Julie recalls her nannies clearly. "Jane and Maureen were the best, but I know I led most of them a bit of a dance. It was really a case of bucking authority, and not just parental authority. The nannies were, after all, a stand-in for my mother, and I played on this and let them know it. I was very resilient, and took one day at a time. There were good and bad days regarding the rows. I, and I think all of us, enjoyed the good days. We did our best to forget about the bad ones. I used to think that they were like a nasty dream and that tomorrow would be good. It often was."

Julie was fond of Maureen's boxer dog, Sheba. "He was so soft and gentle", she said, "but one day I heard him yelping. I went to investigate and found my brother Tim, who was only a toddler then, biting Sheba's ear!

"Jane, our first nanny, was a friend of the family. She had a boy friend called Dave, whom she later married. There were other nannies I remember. One was a little old lady who was bordering on a hypochondriac. One day she fell down the stairs. She didn't seriously hurt herself, but did sustain a few bruises, mostly on her bottom. She used to embarrass everyone, especially my father, by showing her bruises to anyone who came. Suddenly she'd pull up her clothes, drop her panties and show them the bruises on her bottom! It was hilarious.

"Another nanny was an alcoholic. Of course I didn't realise this at the time. She was very well spoken, a highly educated woman, but I don't think she could come to terms with being a nanny. And she used to get drunk, come home reeling, and try to flirt with dad!"

Ruby recalls some differences with nannies when the children were very small. "We had one who used to frighten me silly by saying 'I love the children so much, one day you'll come back and find them gone.' Imagine going off to do a show with that in your mind! Our friend Paul Burnet, the conductor I often toured with, nicknamed her 'The Chinese Prime Minister' because of her inscrutable expression. It was very worrying."

"The Chinese Prime Minister" did at least look after Julie and Tim; but one nanny, who only lasted a week in the Burgess household, expected to be waited on. Ruby found herself cooking and cleaning for the nanny, who justified her job by taking the children to the pictures every day.

When Ruby was working in the north and living at home, Jean and Peter Barbour's house became a sanctuary when she needed one. These were the stilt walkers she and Bernie had met during the tour of *Snow White*, and they became close friends. Ruby used to climb out of the bedroom window, often with her daughter's help, drop the 7ft to the ground and go to them for coffee and comfort. Laughter is never far away from Ruby, and she said: "The first time I jumped from the window I landed right in a large clump of stinging nettles. I had them out pretty smartly."

Soon Julie was also climbing through the window, with her mother's help, because Bernie felt jeans were not suitable wear for her and she wanted to be like her friends who all wore jeans and thick-soled shoes.

"My bedroom was in the wing of the house, a bit that had been built on", Julie recalls. "The window overlooked an alley and eventually that was the one we used. I found a small ladder and kept it handy. That was much easier. I think now it was our own fault we resorted to this. We should have been stronger and said 'Hey, look, this is silly!' Dad's attitude, his strictness, and our fear of that attitude made us devious. I don't want to do him down. I understand him much better now. He has great strength of will and he looked after us well."

When she was older Julie did, in fact, leave home, "The Victorian style of discipline was too strong to take", she says, "but now we are friends."

Life wasn't all doom and gloom, although at the back of the laughter Ruby generated at the parties she loved when away on tour, was the longing for a happy family life. There was great camaraderie among her fellow artistes, and always something happening to provoke a smile.

She used to be known as "the queen of safety pins" when she wore full dresses with lots of petticoats underneath them. One day on stage, stately as a princess, she felt the elastic give in the petticoats and while she stood at the microphone, singing her heart out, they slowly, slowly slipped down to her ankles. Still singing, Ruby stepped out of them, bent down and picked them up, then walked towards the wings to hand them over. Being away from the microphone her voice all but disappeared for a few seconds, but the audience were having such fun it didn't matter. "It was after that episode that I earned my nickname. I always carried safety pins and used a couple to pin the slips to the skirt of the dress and not rely entirely on the elastic. But that night I went from being round and plump to long and thin very quickly!"

Safety pins weren't much use to her the day she drove off to do some shopping. "I usually wear trousers for driving, and I undid the top button for comfort. When I stopped and alighted from the car I completely forgot, took a few steps and down they came, leaving me standing in the centre of a very busy street in my pants!"

Ruby's voice has a limited range, as she is the first to tell you. "It's peculiar really", she says. "Most people when they reach their highest note — mine would be C above middle C, which is not very high — then move into a different voice and carry on. I don't, simply because I have nothing above. When I reach that point that's it, that's the lot. I don't go very low either; my range is about an octave and four notes below, which is quite limited. Sometimes before I go on I'm not sure if anything's going to come out. Most of that is nerves, I know, and I go on and it does." Crossing her fingers, Ruby adds: "Thank heaven!"

In the early days she found it hard to get established with the older stars. "I desperately wanted to be one of them. I so badly wanted them to say 'She's a pro.' Instead I used to hear

'Two-day wonder, give her two years', from some quarters, which was fair comment. We all have to prove ourselves, and I yearned to be accepted by them. Eventually I was, and that made me very happy.

"In the old days there were often comparisons to Vera Lynn, Anne Shelton, and others, and I honestly think it's a great privilege to be compared with them, because to me they were, and are, the best. I grew up on their records, and when I met them I was over the moon. I don't know Vera Lynn well, I've met her about twice in my life. But Anne Shelton and I were friends and I knew her much better, and admired her very much. Anne was the only person for whom I would queue to get an autograph. She used to come to the stage door, and she gave me a signed photograph once. I thought she was magnificent and to have met and worked with people like Anne was a wonderful thing for me." Ruby was devastated when Anne died on 31st July 1994.

Ruby was born under the sign of Aries (The Ram). These people are often deeply sentimental, always chasing a dream, unbelievably idealistic, and put their loved ones on a pedestal. All of these characteristics fit her. Aries people are also said to be demanding, selfish but gentle, and co-operative if met half-way. They are reputed to admire strength, both physical and mental. Most of this rings true in many areas for Ruby. "I think I am a bit weak really, when it comes to standing on my own feet. My mother always says I'm weak. She says 'Why don't you stand up and fight?' but the point is I don't want to fight. I don't want to get aggressive with people, because it's not in me, it's just not in me."

She enjoys painting and is very good, preferring delicate pastels to flamboyant colours. She began doing this when she was on tour in the early Fifties, and Val Doonican had a hand in teaching her.

"It was at the height of my crush on Val, although I don't think he realised how lovesick I was. I did try not to wear my heart too obviously on my sleeve, not always successfully I admit. Val used to paint, he's a very good artist. When I expressed interest he gave me some lessons. I've painted, on and off, ever since. It's a soothing occupation and I find it a great tension-reliever."

She admits that long periods elapse without her putting brush to canvas, and then, in her usual all-or-nothing fashion, she paints for days or weeks, as though there were no tomorrow. Her subjects are often elves, fairies, "the wee folk", the fantasy creatures.

"If I had to choose one luxury item to take on a desert island, were I to be stranded there, it would be my paints, brushes and lots of canvasses. But as to escaping; no, I don't think so. I'd be pretty hopeless at building a boat!"

In 1974 Ruby filed for divorce. She and Bernie were still together when she wasn't touring, but arguing most of the time. Because they both very much wanted to make a go of their marriage, they talked again and decided to give it another try. Bernie wanted her to give up showbusiness, but this was the one thing she wouldn't do. "My work has always meant a lot to me", she said, "and with all the unhappiness I relied on it even more. The friction was there, whether I was working or not."

In spite of both their good intentions, the arguments went on and even became worse. Temperamentally they were so different. "When we worked together we could just about cope, but not otherwise", Ruby said. Bernie liked the management side of showbusiness now he was so involved with it, and his organised and tidy nature were great assets. All Ruby asked was to be able to sing. Ideally she would have liked her family travelling with her, but was realistic enough to acknowledge that staying home with Bernie meant the children had regular schooling, and a proper home. "I never had any doubts that they were well looked after, but the selfish side of me missed them", she said.

CHAPTER 15

Just a little drink...

Lee Stevens and David Frankish had booked Ruby for some club dates in Yorkshire about this time. The domestic situation was worsening and she was drinking heavily, as well as taking valium to calm her nerves. She knew she shouldn't mix the two, but on her way to a booking in Halifax, after a stupendous row with Bernie, she was sitting on the back seat of the car drinking vodka.

She did go on and did her full 45 minutes, but she says: "It was terrible because I was like a zombie, completely without the physical energy necessary to perform properly. I have no actual memory of going on stage, or of anything until I woke up in bed the following afternoon."

The whole episode shamed and distressed her so much that she gave the promoters their money back, and in a state of high nervous tension, went on to play the other clubs she was booked for. The rest of the week went well. Ruby admits she took a couple of drinks for "Dutch courage" before going on. The following Saturday, for her final concerts on that circuit, her car arrived very late and as she was playing two venues, it threw the whole evening's timing out. At the first place the accompanist played by ear and there wasn't time to rehearse.

"Someone who plays by ear can be brilliant, but that doesn't mean they can accompany you unless they know all your music by heart. There you are waiting for cues for key changes, and when they don't come you're lost", Ruby said, "Fate or something or Someone was on my side, because the audience could tell that the pianist and I weren't synchronising, and that I was trying not to let it show, and they gave me a wonderful ovation, turning what I thought would be a nightmare into something approaching a success."

At the second club the concert got off to an unsteady start because of her lateness. The place was packed with tables right up to the stage, which frightened her. The audience, fed up with waiting, were doing a slow handclap and the compere of the show announced her by saying "Ruby Murray has finally arrived", which didn't help matters. But Ruby is not without a lot of courage, and, quivering inside her flimsy dress, she took a deep breath and began.

"I could feel the animosity", she said. "The first three numbers and my bit of Irish patter died. Yet I had to get through to them, and somehow, I still don't know how, but by the fourth song I felt the warmth coming at me, slowly at first but, my goodness, how it encouraged me." When the show finished she had the biggest ovation of the entire week. "They must have read the Press reports about Monday night", she said, "and my lateness probably confirmed their fears, but they were generous enough to allow me to win them over. It was a small victory, but one I needed desperately and I was grateful."

After that awful week Ruby cancelled future bookings until she had sorted herself out. A paragraph in some of the papers said she was ill, and she finally admitted that fact to herself. Her drinking had grown beyond her own ability to stop.

Trumpeter Freddie Clayton, who had written a book called *The Alcohol Problem Explained: Stop Drinking and Start Living*, wrote to her to say he'd heard she was in trouble with her drinking and would like to offer support. Bernie also welcomed anything that would help. "I must have been hell to live with at that time", she said. Freddie visited them at Rectory Cottage, and then he introduced her to Alcoholics Anonymous. Ruby attended three AA meetings, to which Bernie took her, and says: "I can't pretend the experience was a success, because I simply was not able to get up as an anonymous person and explain my problem before a packed audience. And, famous or not, my voice is kind of unmistakable. Everyone there knew me, and I was in such a state of nerves I found I couldn't bare my soul. It's a marvellous organisation, but it wasn't what I needed then". Her doctor agreed that her problems needed sorting out. "You are ill", he said. "Accept that and then we can do something about it." Ruby recalls: "I was crying a lot, over-crying, and I had to talk my life through with the psychiatrist, who said I needed treatment." She and Bernie agreed, and Dr. Tozland, "a marvellous man", booked her into St. Andrew's, a private hospital in Northampton where she was under the care of Dr. Michael Brook.

"The first thing they did was put me to sleep for two days because my mind was over-active. I couldn't still it. I was distressed all the time, so I had this complete rest, no telephone calls or anything because it's a cutaway from the outside world to allow your mind to rest. Actually I felt awful the first night. The nurse said, 'I'll give you your tablets, don't lock yourself in your room, you're not mad', and of course that's the first thing I did. 'Don't cry', she said, and of course I did that too. I locked the door, started to cry and thought, I'm mad. I felt so lonely. She said, 'You'll feel better after a couple of days. You'll get used to people and you'll be able to straighten yourself out.' Then the tablets began to work and I slept."

Ruby was in St. Andrew's for a month. "It was funny", she said, "because I went down to breakfast, which I don't eat as a rule. But after the initial two days you were expected to make an effort and go down. There were marvellous people there, doctors, headmasters, all highly intelligent people, and we were all suffering from stress and I found I could talk a bit about it. We were encouraged to talk things out.

"After a week or two I didn't want to leave. It wasn't a prison; they had dances, swimming pools, all kinds of entertainment. You could have a drink if you wanted one. It was a sheltered life, a cocoon. I had to have injections and I've always been terrified of the needle, but I wanted so much to get better and I went along with everything that was prescribed. At first I was not allowed telephone calls, and then as the days went by only the minimum contact with the outside world; and the strange thing was, at least it seemed strange to me then, I was happy there."

After the initial isolation, Bernie visited her twice, the second time taking Tim with him. Julie, who was 12, was very concerned about her mother and used to skip school sometimes and walk six miles to visit and spend the day with her.

Ruby did a couple of paintings while she was there, read a lot, and ate properly, something she hadn't been doing when she was drinking heavily. Before she left, the doctor said: "You're fine now, but you're going back to the same environment. Don't think things have changed, because they probably haven't." This proved true, but she returned to Rectory Cottage and tried again, and within two years she had another breakdown and was back in St. Andrew's.

Bernie and Ruby knew then they would have to part. "We were increasingly unhappy, rowing in front of the children; not physical violence, although that sometimes happened when we were in bed or when Bernie came in from work at the club in the small hours and found me downstairs drunk and crying. I'd hit out in my intoxicated state and be so terribly sorry afterwards." Bernie wouldn't leave the home, his work was there, and it was a stable base for the children. Ruby's doctor told her. "You'll have to leave. It's a lovely house, I know, but it's going to kill you if you don't. And you'll have to go without your children." She says: "This was hard, probably one of the hardest decisions I've had to make. But I left."

She packed two suitcases, one containing her stage dresses and music, the other her personal clothes and mementoes, and she went to see Ray in Torquay. She had been seeing him fairly often during the last few years, and they set up home together.

But let Ruby tell you of her feelings at this time...

"I think the week in the Yorkshire clubs really brought it home to me. Of course I knew I was drinking far too much, but until then it hadn't been obvious. It hadn't affected my work, although I think some managements were wary about booking me in case I'd been on the bottle.

"How can I give a reason? Perhaps it's in my blood. They do say everyone has the potential to become an alcoholic the same as everyone has the potential to develop certain illnesses. And if the conditions are right for it...

"In the world of showbusiness it's easy to get into a drinking pattern. The tour I did with dear David Whitfield, for instance. It was a month of one-night stands, and I never could say no when the fans wanted to buy me a drink afterwards. I was lonely for Bernie. I need a man around, and he wasn't there. It wasn't entirely his fault, because he had just been appointed manager of the New Cresta Club. But now I'm making excuses and that's no good either. The plain truth is that I was so very unhappy and I turned to drink. It wasn't the answer. It helped dull the pain but it couldn't make it go away. But it took me out of myself for a few hours, and I came to depend on it more and more. It was a refuge, a hiding place for the rejection I felt.

"Twice I filed for divorce, then withdrew so we could try again. The second time, in 1974, Bernie took counter-action saying I physically attacked him on a number of occasions. This was true. Frustrated beyond words because I couldn't explain what was happening, because I'm on an emotional see-saw most of the time and he is not, I hit out with whatever was to hand. I'm not proud of that. Bernie and I loved each other, but we were complete opposites in temperament. Our ideas of what was important were poles apart, and this affected everything, from bringing up the children to choosing our friends. In those days I wore my heart on my sleeve. Bernie hid his behind barbed wire. We tried again several times but it never worked; behind the happy family image seen by the public was quarrelling, bitterness and frustration.

"I withdrew my divorce petition in 1974 because of the children. I didn't want a legal battle, and I tried to make my marriage work. It was a vicious circle. I was still on the bottle, the rows continued and each time that sent me back to it. The doctor prescribed tablets for depression, and I took to bringing bottles of drink into the house and hiding them so I'd always have some.

"Eventually we were living in the same house but leading separate lives. I embarked on one or two affairs; it was good to feel wanted again. Always it was with a man who made me laugh, and for whom I felt a great affection. Of course I told myself it was love each time, on my part anyway. I was working hard, yes, and still drinking hard; but I managed to keep off it before a show. Music and singing are very important to me and I didn't want to lose them; I knew the answer was in my own hands, but it wasn't easy. The affairs helped, too — in a way they restored my battered self esteem.

"I had met Ray Lamar again when I was working at Festival Hall, Paignton, in 1973 and from then on we saw each other regularly. My work took me all around the country, and every time I was in the south-west Ray and I got together. His second marriage was in difficulties, my marriage was over in everything but name... I dashed between Wootton and Torquay, working, loving the children, worrying, drinking... Where had I gone so terribly wrong? Why? I had only ever wanted a loving relationship; it seemed to me I'd been searching for this all my life. After my second stint in St. Andrew's I packed my cases and joined Ray in Torquay."

In 1977 Ruby and Bernie divorced. He had custody of the children, with which she was in full agreement. They were both still at school and the lawyer told her: "There's no way they'll let you take them touring." She had to keep on singing, partly for her own sanity and partly for financial reaons. She was hurt by criticisms that she had left them, and now says: "I took the brunt from the public for leaving my children, but there was no way I could take them with me. When they left school they came down. Julie got a job as a bluecoat at Pontins and a few years later, when Tim left school, he did too."

Both Julie and Tim are good singers. Critic Barry Balmayne, writing in *The Stage* recently after watching Tim, says: "I am of the age bracket to have been educated to listen to, and enjoy, the lyrics of a good song. Quite regularly these days I need an interpreter alongside me to establish both the words and the story.

Not so with Tim Murray who competely restored my faith in younger generation vocalists when I caught his act in Northampton. I am totally confident that, as he matures even more, his name and fame will rise with him to great heights in show business. Already he is a good-looking, modern young man with all the basic ingredients for success."

Both Bernie and Ruby were delighted with that write-up, to say nothing of Tim himself. In 1989 Tim won his heat in the TV talent show *New Faces*, and came fifth in the final. He returned to Pontins in the summer of 1989 as the cabaret star, and Ruby was there to watch and encourage. She was nervous for him — on the surface, more so than he was — but she was also very, very proud as he wooed and won his audience.

Julie is a bar manageress in a night-club, and recently when Ruby was working in the area she walked in after her show. Julie says: "The barman came to tell me 'Your mother's at the bar', and I said, 'And the Flying Scotsman's just left.' He did his best to convince me, then returned to his work. A few moments later he was back, 'Your mother's having a drink at the bar', he said. I walked through, and there she was, in full stage make-up and dress, looking absolutely gorgeous and laughing. 'You didn't believe him, did you?' she said. It was a big thrill to see her there and it made me glow."

She admits she would have liked to have seen more of her mother when she was younger, "but she's the best mother in the world and I idolised her. I wasn't envious of other childrens' family lives. I think I was a naturally resilient personality. I went through a stage of not getting on, as so many do. But it wasn't for long, and now we're the best of pals."

Julie also sees Bernie. For a time they clashed badly: "I don't agree with everything he says, but I do understand more now. Once, when I was fighting him over something, I remember him saying some words from a song Perry Como used to sing. 'If you have a son, you worry; if you have a daughter, you pray.' That moved me very much."

CHAPTER 16

The Great Escape

Divorce is like a little death", Ruby said, "added to which I felt I had failed. I know now, I can see, that we were never right for each other, but when you're first in love you don't look for the snags. It wasn't anybody's fault..."

In 1985 Ruby appeared with a host of other stars in the *Forty Years Of Peace* programme and there she met yet another member of the Royal Family, Princess Anne. "A super person, such a lovely personality", she says. It was a happy reunion time with many colleagues, among them Harry Secombe with whom she had last worked 27 years ago. He, remembering their duet in Yarmouth, mimed *If You Were The Only Girl in the World* from his position on stage to hers, and she was thrilled he had remembered.

Harry also recalled the time when Ruby was rushing from the Palladium for a cabaret appearance. She used to go by tube. "It was fun in those days", she said, "and no-one took any notice of a girl in evening dress on the Tube because most of us really dressed up when we went anywhere special."

On this particular occasion, however, she, Harry Secombe and her agent Keith Devon, were going down the escalator when the draught created as a train rushed through the station blew her full skirt up. Hastily patting it down, she didn't see it catch at the bottom of the staircase — and as she stepped off there was a ripping sound. She left a good deal of the dress behind.

It was at Bridlington in 1967 that her dress, this time a tight fitting red one, caught on the moving carousel as it took the artistes round for their final bow. Not realising this, Ruby stepped off to walk to the front of the stage as it slowed down.

Vince Hill's quick reaction saved a nasty accident. He leapt from his "galloper", clambered over three more horses to reach Ruby's, and lifted her off. That incident also left the bottom of her dress caught in the mechanism, but at least her flesh was intact.

Her speed at closing a car door once shut her pianist's hand in it. This was Dennis Plowright who played for her on tour. Fortunately he didn't break any bones or do permanent damage to his hand, and Ruby was more upset about the incident than he was.

A few years ago she did a cabaret season at Pontin's Holiday Camp in Brixham, just a few miles from her home, and on the last night she had had a row with Ray. Chris Chambers, manager of the camp, persuaded her to stay on. About two hours later Ruby's temper had cooled, but when she started to leave she found they had taken all her clothes and her car keys.

"They took a bit of a shine to me and didn't think Ray was right. 'See how you feel in a couple of days', they said." And Ruby was virtually a prisoner in the camp, because they had warned all the bluecoats not to let her near a telephone. Each time she managed it and started to dial, a hand would descend on her shoulder, and when she looked round there would be a bluecoat shaking his head.

So she made herself rise at 2am (not easy for Ruby) to phone Ray. When she couldn't get him she tried the Queen's Hotel where she knew the night porter Joe. "Please contact Ray and ask him to come and get me", she pleaded. "I'm going mad and I can't get out. Tell him I'll be outside the main gate at five o'clock this morning."

Ray contacted another friend, ex-boxer Paul King, and together they went to Brixham as dawn was breaking.

Meanwhile, back at the camp, Ruby took off her shoes and crept out. She avoided the paths and went through the trees to evade detection. Then she went down on her knees in the undergrowth, past the security guard, and finally out into the road. Paul's Jaguar slid quietly to a halt beside her within minutes, and shivering she got in and they drove back to Torquay. They returned the following day because her music and stage clothes were still there, and she stayed in the car while Ray went in to collect them. It says something about all of their personalities that they are still friends, and refer to it as "The Great Escape".

Another story she likes to tell is about the time she was on *This Is Your Life*, when Katie Boyle was the "victim". Katie had been in the first television series Ruby did, *Quite Contrary*, and the *This Is Your Life* researchers had therefore asked Ruby to be one of the guests to greet Katie. Ruby was, of course, sworn to secrecy, and she went to London early so she could have her hair done before the show. She had it permed for the first time in her life, and spent the rest of the day trying to get it to go her way because she didn't like it at all. She did the show, just walking on and saying "Hullo, lovely to see you", and the following day, when she was talking to her mother on the phone, she told her she had been a guest on a *This Is Your Life* programme, (without saying whose life), and had had her hair cut and permed for the occasion. "But it looks awful", she added, "I don't like it one bit."

Winnie said: "Jesus, what did you do that for?" And Ruby answered truthfully: "I don't know. I thought it would look nice short. It was just a brainstorm."

Winnie asked: "When does the programme come out? I'll watch."

"September."

"September? That's months away. What are you worrying about, girl. It'll have grown by then!"

Barbara Kelly "got it in one" when Ruby was the mystery guest in the early days of *What's My Line*.

Ruby spent weeks cultivating her English accent, and duly went on and signed in. Eamonn Andrews gave Barbara the first question and she asked: "Are you in showbiz?"

Ruby said, "Yes" in her best English voice, and Barbara said: "Ruby Murray!" It was one of the quickest solutions in the history of the show.

Ruby still laughs about her slip of the tongue when she was making a speech to The Blind Association, and said; "On behalf of the blind dogs for the guides ... "

She has done a lot of charity work. All the proceeds from her recording of *You've Got To Have Heart* went to the Heart Foundation, and she has raised so much money for the Guide Dog association that they have named a dog after her. "I'm enormously pleased of course, but it does tickle me to imagine a dog called Ruby", she said.

In the spring of 1981 she was at the Hotel Tara on St. Patrick's Night for the Save The Children Fund. She was due to begin at 9.30pm, but the preceding fashion show over-ran to the extent of two hours. Always nervous before a performance, Ruby felt sick with anxiety, but her professionalism and her natural charm revived that flagging audience.

Steve Absolom, writing in *The Stage,* said: "The Irish star had need of all her resources of charm and humour to surmount the disadvantages of a two-hour delay in starting. Happily all went well. Ruby Murray has now left 'the little colleen next door' so far behind her that she can stun in sequinned turquoise chiffon and a long blonde hair-do that challenges Dolly Parton at her own game, without for a second losing the husky catch in her voice that catapulted her to the top of the charts in the Fifties. She has matured in expertise, and now presents a polished and well planned act."

Ruby has also done a lot of work for the mentally handicapped and for Lions clubs around Britain. She flew to Ireland to do a show with Frank Carson for the mentally handicapped on the day of the Enniskillen Remembrance Day bomb disaster.

The Irish troubles never cease to worry her. "If only everyone could live in peace with everyone else, but I know from experience it isn't always possible within a family, let alone within a country."

She is still deeply in love with Ireland, but it's the Ireland of her childhood that she dreams about. "From the moment I set foot in England I loved her", she says, "and this part where we now live is best of all. It has everything; sea, country, town, good climate, and a fascinating history.

"For many years Torquay didn't have a theatre at all, but in 1880 a Dr. Gillow turned the old Assembly Room into one, and many famous and worthy actors and actresses have played there. In 1886 the Princesss of Wales visited with her daughters, and according to reports of the time the Royal Box was decorated with blue ribbons, lace and velvet, and the royal party saw two plays, *Kerry* and *In Chancery*, performed by Edward Terry and his company."

Ruby loves to find out about these things. "That's when the title Royal was added to the theatre. Sadly it ceased to present live entertainment in 1933 and became the Odeon Cinema."

The Princess Theatre — the former Pavilion Theatre — on the seafront, has seen so many wonderful stars on its stage. It has been converted into an excellent leisure centre but still presents the cream of showbusiness. The theatre, albeit smaller, still exists within.

Ruby's mother, Winnie, died in 1989. She used to visit a couple of times a year; Ray, who loves the West country, always drove to London to fetch her. On one occasion, when they reached the Devon border, Ray sighed happily and said: "Ah, back to lovely, peaceful Devon". That night there was a great storm, a fire in a hotel... and in the morning Winnie said pithily: "*Peaceful* Devon, with the wind whistling, the fire engines dashing by, the police sirens blaring, and the pubs turning out! Give me London any day..."

For three of Ruby's fans, a weekend in Torquay staying with her is a highlight in their year. "The girls", Ruby calls them affectionately, and they all met originally at various stage doors after one of Ruby's shows.

"There were eight of us to begin with", says one of them, Joyce Wiles, "and we met for weekends and holidays wherever Ruby was appearing. To make sure we had our money's worth we used to book tickets for every night of our stay.

"Looking back, there must have been times when she thought we were haunting her. But if we annoyed her she never let it show. She was the same towards us whenever and wherever we saw her. There was always a chat and a smile as we waded through our inevitable autographs and she said many times, 'Thank you for being so loyal, it means a lot to me.'"

Celia Hydon recalls the first time she saw Ruby in person. It was in 1955 at Coventry. She went along to the stage door after the show in the hope of getting her autograph. "There were hundreds of people there", she said. "Within minutes of the show finishing the area was crowded and the police were there to control it. There was no way Ruby could have come out, so the police got the crowd into a line about six-deep and let them in a few at a time. Ruby sat at a table behind a window, signing autographs and photographs, but she spoke to everyone. I didn't have an autograph book at that time so she signed a piece of paper for me. I still have that piece of paper."

Later Celia won a fan club competition and had her first private meeting with her idol. The competition was to find who had the most photographs of her. "I was a bit dubious about sending my collection through the post for fear of losing it", she said, "but eventually I risked it." The prize was two tickets for the show and a dressing room meeting with Ruby when she was next in the winner's area. Celia said she was very nervous when it came to the point, but "Ruby was great and soon put me at ease."

When the eight of them were going on holiday together to Margate for two weeks they did their usual thing and booked eight front row seats for the entire fortnight. Hughie Green was also on the bill, and they soon discovered that he went to one particular seat every night, the spotlight following him there, and asked the occupant to stand up and try to take a trick paper flower from him. "We were stuck with it for a few days, then we drew lots and that seat was always empty until it was safe in the second half", Joyce said.

At Sutton Coldfield, a magician was on the bill. Ruby had gone out during the first half, when she didn't appear, to get something to eat, and the girls were happily enjoying the show until the magician came down and took them back on stage with him as rather reluctant participants for his act. Joyce says: "As if it wasn't bad enough entertaining the audience while being made to look extremely foolish it didn't help to see Ruby at the back absolutely doubled up with laughter. She'd got back just in time to catch our act."

Another time they all recall with laughter was in the Isle of Man. They were with Ruby and some others after the show, having chicken and chips in a basket. Celia was eating and talking, eating and talking, and when the others had almost finished her basket seemed to be fuller than ever. As she looked at it Ruby's hand came over and dropped another chicken bone in. She had thought that one was the waste basket! "We didn't choke on chicken bones that night, but we nearly choked with laughter", Celia said.

June Snook joined Ruby's fan club in 1955, and met her idol for the first time on a club trip to Brighton, where she was doing a summer season.

"There were so many people trying to get near her, all I had a chance to say was Hello, but she was so friendly with everyone and never seemed to tire of smiling and signing autographs. From that time on I travelled all over the country whenever I could to see her. And after the show I would go round to the stage door of whatever theatre it was and join hundreds of other fans waiting for her to come out.

"I met Celia and Joyce, and the three of us used to spend our holidays wherever Ruby was doing a summer season. One year, around Christmas-time, Ruby invited eight of us to Rectory Cottage. She cooked us a meal. It really was a dream come true to be there, and hard to believe we were being entertained in Ruby's home. After a lovely evening, Bernie took us back to Northampton, where we stayed the night before going our separate ways the following morning."

Ruby remembers a time in Jersey when the three friends had come over for the weekend, and she persuaded them to stay another day because the weather was so good and she wanted them to enjoy themselves. "There were phone calls to husbands, because they were married by then, and booking in to the boarding house for another night and I thought 'What if it pours with rain tomorrow after all? They'll wish they'd gone home!' It didn't — and they didn't."

Celia summed up the relationship for all of them: "It's not a case of star meets fan, but friend meets friend."

CHAPTER 17

Irish eyes are smiling

In 1982 Ruby was in a local pub in Torquay. It was a party, and someone slipped a "Micky Finn" into her drink. When they came out and walked along the front to return home she was singing and very merry. They went past a stationary police vehicle and Ruby called out and tapped on the windows. Then she drummed a tune on the windows with her fingers and called to them again. And a young police constable got out of the vehicle and arrested her. He took her to the police station and put her in a cell, where she passed out. In the middle of the night she woke, and was terrified. "It was a dreadful experience", she said, "and I felt so ashamed."

When she had sobered up they couldn't let her out because she had been charged. Growing bored within the confines of the cell she gave the officers on duty their own private concert through the bars. This illustrates so well her mercurial nature, but it didn't mean she wasn't worried. Simply, to use her own words, that she "kept on going on".

She had to appear in court and was fined £30. "It was a very dark point", she says, "but worst of all was the family. I felt so awful letting everyone down like that." She telephoned her mother to apologise, and also her children. She was crying when she phoned Tim and he said: "It's all right, mum, it's great. I'm ever so popular, none of the others have a mum whose been in jail!"

"He made light of it", she said, "which was dear of him, but I never want to get out of control again." The newspapers naturally enough latched on to this episode, and in some cases made headlines out of it:

"Singer Ruby Murray broke down and wept yesterday when

she was fined £30 for being drunk and disorderly. Magistrates in Devon heard that Miss Murray was arrested outside her home on Saturday night after shouting at passers-by. Her Fifties hits included the million-seller, *Softly, Softly.*"

It was good journalism contrasting *Softly, Softly*, and shouting at passers-by, but it hurt Ruby deeply. "It was just a Saturday night party. I had had too much to drink, but the Micky Finn was a cruel thing to do. Even so, had it been anyone else you probably wouldn't have heard any more about it", she says now, "or only a paragraph if they were very short of news."

Some years later she met Detective-Inspector Geoff Bates, who was the sergeant on duty at the station the night she was booked for being drunk and disorderly. He asked her forgiveness. "Do you know", he said, "my mother didn't speak to me for a month afterwards because she said I should have let you go!"

When the court case was over Ray took her away for a few days holiday because she was brooding about it so. They went to a pub in Wiltshire, on the Longleat Estate. Ray knew Lord Bath from the days when he used to get him seats for the pantomime at the Bristol Hippodrome, and during their stay on the Somerset/Wiltshire border they were invited to dinner at Longleat.

Ruby, whose spirits are up and down like quicksilver, threw herself into the atmosphere and enjoyed the beauty of the great estate. "It was a bonus going to the private apartments the public don't see", she said, "and we were able to look at handwritten letters from Queen Elizabeth I and Sir Walter Raleigh The sense of history and permanence was spine-tingling. And we met most of the family, who were charming to us.

"When one of the sons took us to his private apartments and showed us his paintings — murals on the wall and ceilings, of nudes in every conceivable position — he asked what I thought. Well, I didn't know what to say for a moment", (her accent becomes even more pronounced when she is telling a story). "I could hardly say it's lovely, so I said, 'Well, it's interesting, very interesting.'"

She wanted now more than anything to forget the incident, to block it out completely, but she was booked for more dates and she knew everyone would have read about her lapse. Courageously she introduced it herself in those first few shows afterwards: "Ladies and gentlemen, there's something you ought to know. I haven't got a cold, I haven't got a sore throat, I just speak like this so there's no need any of us worrying about it. Truth is my mother left me out in the rain when I was a baby and I got rusted up. God love her, I think she likes a drop of the hard stuff and any of you who read the *Sunday People* will be thinking I take after her..." The chords from the piano increased and then she was into her first number, *Everywhere you go, sunshine follows you...*

In fact it was her father and not her mother who "liked a few jars", says Ruby: "One of the anti-things when I had money was that he could afford more drink, and that was very sad, but I couldn't not have made sure the family had enough money."

One of the stories Ruby tells about the Palladium days of *Painting The Town* is of Big Dan and his pride in her. "He used to go to the pub in the time between first and second house and when the crowds from the first performance came in he'd listen to them talking, and if they said, 'Isn't she lovely?' it would be 'Buy the whole bar a drink, buy everybody a drink!' (with my money, you know). By the same token if he heard anyone say, 'Well, I don't know what all the fuss is about, I don't think she's all that great', he had them by the scruff of the neck and then there was a fight. 'Are you talking about my daughter?' he'd roar.

"He was a great man, and he loved me being famous. He showed off like mad about me, and it could be embarrassing. But then he was my dad and that was his way."

She speaks frankly and quietly about her drinking. "Back in the Fifties I never touched it; a cup of tea was my tipple then."

Her eyes twinkle as she adds: "I still enjoy a good cuppa but, yes, the drink was a problem for a while. At first it helped me forget the unhappinesses and the pressures, and of course it was easily available at most after-the-show parties. But, as I said earlier, it doesn't solve the problems, only adds to them. You have to be strong and it is often difficult, but I'd tell people that it can be done..."

Ruby and Ray married in 1993. Ruby has lived in Torquay now for 15 years; Ray of course, has lived there much longer. She has known riches, and she has enjoyed it: "I always knew I would sing, but I never dreamed it would happen as it did. I'm proud to have achieved so much, it would be silly and untrue to say otherwise, and I'm fortunate that I still keep busy."

Because she started so young, and was at the top of the tree at 19 a lot of people think she is older than she is. One afternoon she was waiting for Ray in the hotel where she was to appear in cabaret that evening when she heard two people seated at a table somewhere behind her, talking. "Ruby Murray's on tonight. I always liked her. Mind, she must be in her seventies now because I remember her when I was a girl." Her companion said: "So do I. But she doesn't look anything like that in the photographs outside. Perhaps they're old ones." When Ray appeared and they went outside Ruby stopped and looked at the stills. "Come on, love, you've seen them before", Ray was impatient. "I know, but I just wanted to check." Ruby laughed. "I'm glad we didn't use old publicity", she said, "I'll tell you why later."

She still loves meeting her audience after her shows — possibly more now than in earlier times because she isn't as shy and there is more time to talk. Many of them know she's been through the mill a bit, and they admire the way she's fought back. But the main ingredient of her shows today is her ever-present talent.

Her voice has always been soft, husky, a ballad singer's voice; these days it has the experience of suffering in it, too. She is a gentle person (most of the time). "I'm certainly no saint, and I wouldn't like people to think that", she says, "but I've never deliberately hurt anyone in my life."

She likes luxury, good food, good wine, good conversation and good friends. "I love love; I suppose I'm still a bit in love with love." And she still dreams, but underlying it all now is a seasoning of reality.

To this day she cannot read music, and makes her own marks on her band parts, to the amusement of her accompanist — be it pianist, trio or full orchestra. But she has an innate sense of music, of rhythm, and of timing.

She has been in showbusiness for 40 years, and for most of that time she has been in work. The comparatively few years at the highest point of the pyramid are maintained by her steady workload since. In her particular branch of the profession that is not an easy achievement. In the legitimate theatre an actor or actress can start playing juveniles and go on to second lead and lead. Then they must depend on their drawing power, because only a handful of them can transcend age, style and topicality. Then there are the character parts — some marvellous ones. But in the world of variety everything hinges on one person's drawing power. In the straight theatre an actress is part of a team with her act. In variety she is on her own.

The Beverley Sisters and Dorothy Squires aren't alone when they talk about a television show for Ruby. Author Michael Thornton says: "I have always felt that if only someone could come up with the right comedy role, or even the right dramatic role, she could well have a whole new career as a character actress. Her timing is impeccable."

Ruby's answer to that is: "Why not? I enjoy a bit of banter with my audience and maybe it's time for a change of direction."

She is still easily bruised and, although she's learned to hide her feelings, she blossoms when she is surrounded by warm, caring people. She has never wanted, nor expected, star treatment; she loves what she does and enjoys being "one of the people" afterwards. When she was younger she probably needed protection from herself, but her impulsive, wayward nature was against this. "All the people I fell in love with in those days wanted to protect me", she said. "When I wanted passion they offered protection."

In 1985 the American rock star Madonna had three hits in the Top Ten and there was talk of her breaking Ruby's record. Terry Wogan invited Ruby on to his TV show, and for fun she did a Madonna "take-off". She drew a little picture of Terry Wogan on her knees — one on each, of him happy and sad — and says her friends wouldn't let her wash her knees for three weeks! "I had to wash round the drawings until they'd all seen them! It was a laugh."

In the event Madonna didn't break Ruby's record of five hits in the Top Twenty simultaneously — *Softly, Softly* at one, *Heartbeat* at two, *Happy Days and Lonely Nights* at four, *If Anyone Finds This I Love You* at five, and *Evermore* at six. And they all stayed there for 11 weeks; *Softly, Softly* went on for another three.

"It is amazing how the fans still remember me", she says, "but it's lovely too. At the time of the comparison I hadn't heard of Madonna, and I don't suppose she'd heard of me. But I was invited on early morning television, and that was murder... I hate getting up in the morning!"

Ruby says she would not like to return to those top-of-the-bill days — "I don't think I'd have the stamina" — but she is doing what she loves to do, and Ray is there to share, love, and, yes, to protect.

"Ray's had a marvellous career", she says, "He was a terrific dancer when he was younger, one of the best tap dancers in England, and a good musician, too. Then there's all that management experience. He has that quality that can stand back and let everyone make a lot of me. 'She's done well, they love her'. That's what he thinks and he's happy about it and glad for me."

Ruby can look back on a record that has stood for 40 years.

Of the first seven recordings she made, six went into the hit parade, and five into the Top Twenty. And they stayed there long enough to create this unique record for the girl from Belfast. She was a home-loving girl, a romantic lass who was afraid of being left on the shelf (though heaven alone knows why). She never put on airs and graces, and maybe that's part of why she is still so popular with her fellow artistes today.

She came through her drinking problems, scarred but still singing. In 1989 she was booked for a spot in Brixham, sharing top-of-the-bill with John Hanson. She accepted, mainly because it was near enough for her to return home to Torquay each night. But it didn't work out. Ruby was sacked — there were too many stars.

"I have been on time and sober for each performance", she said. "I did what the management wanted. But first one song, then another, was cut, until if you blinked your eye you'd have missed me." That night in May she gave her usual performance and when the curtain came down she was told, "That's it, sorry." The following day she looked smart and fresh. "I've cried all night", she said, "now I'm going to fight. I fulfilled my contract. I kept off the drink."

She was too late now to try for a summer season because everything was booked, but nevertheless she was in work almost throughout. She starred in cabaret, clubs, theatres — once more travelling the land, living out of a suitcase, the very thing she had tried to avoid by taking the Brixham booking. It's been a hard struggle to keep off the drink, and once or twice she hasn't succeeded. There is so much in her life that can send her back to it; but she knows it isn't the answer, and she is determined to fight this particular battle. She has seen what it has done to others in her profession, she knows what it can do to her.

Her voice is good. You still wouldn't hear her at the back without a microphone, but that's no longer a problem. It was in *Snow White* when the taxi messages cut in — modern technology has seen to that.

When Ruby sings you can understand the words, and when she smiles you want to smile back. Her voice has an infectious quality.

She is still either up in the clouds or down in the depths. "I'm never on an even keel, can't find a middle level. It's just the way I am, I suppose." But now she understands it and is much more contented.

Ray says: "I've known and loved Ruby a long, long time. Of course, we have our disagreements like most couples; we're neither of us saints. But after all the upheavals we found happiness together. Now we are devoted to each other."

Ruby isn't a hoarder. She hasn't kept a lot to mark her career at the top. There's a suitcase of photographs and press cuttings, a framed certificate from the Royal Variety Show, a brass nameplate from the star dressing room of the Palladium, and statuettes for being top recording star. But, most of all, she still has her memories. She looks back, with happiness and gratitude, for what she had — and looks forward, with her own inimitable Irish zest, for whatever is in her future.

For details of other tapes available, prices etc. please see overleaf ▶